WORKING DRAWING HANDBOOK
A Guide for Architects and Builders

ROBERT C. McHUGH

VNR **VAN NOSTRAND REINHOLD COMPANY**
NEW YORK   CINCINNATI   ATLANTA   DALLAS   SAN FRANCISCO
LONDON   TORONTO   MELBOURNE

Van Nostrand Reinhold Company Regional Offices:
New York   Cincinnati   Atlanta   Dallas   San Francisco

Van Nostrand Reinhold Company International Offices:
London   Toronto   Melbourne

Manufactured in the United States of America

Published by Van Nostrand Reinhold Company
135 West 50th Street, New York, N.Y. 10020

Published simultaneously in Canada by Van Nostrand Reinhold Ltd.

15 14 13 12 11 10 9 8 7 6 5

Library of Congress Cataloging in Publication Data

McHugh, Robert C.
    Working drawing handbook.

    Includes bibliographical references and index.
    1. Architectural drawing.   I. Title.
NA2700.M32   1977   720'.28   77-23157
ISBN 0-442-25283-8
ISBN 0-442-25284-6 pbk.

The knowledge, inspiration, and encouragement needed to undertake this project came from many sources. Much of the knowledge was the result of experience gained during my career. The inspiration came from a desire to help others learn this work and to find an improved way of accomplishing it. The encouragement came from many people who saw what I was trying to do.

Special energy was received from the following friends: Frank Piermarocchi, who got me started in this exciting field; Jack Zeiler, who helped me see all of the ways in which drawings are used; Rod Mager, who helped in the initial phases of research; Lincoln Jones, who put up with me while I tested my theories out on his projects; Dick McHugh, who encouraged me to put this information into a usable form; Tom DeAngelo, my dad, John Barnett, Mike Lackey, Ashley Chase, and J. R. Johnson, all of whom were involved in proofreading the rough draft; Polly Specht and Ione Woog, who typed the manuscript over and over again; and Lena Walker, who assisted on publication revisions.

ACKNOWLEDGMENTS

to Mary...

This is a handbook which describes an approach to producing working drawings. It is written for architects, students, and builders.

Working drawings are the visual aids which a designer uses to communicate his ideas to builders. The terms "plans" and "specifications" may be more familiar to the layman.

Many decisions must be made during the construction process. In the typical situation, the designer is not at the job site to make them. Even if he were, he could not fulfill this need quickly and sensibly enough to keep the process in motion. The working drawings eliminate this gap in communication.

To fulfill such a role, they must be clear, complete, and correct. They must guide the builder in his production of the ideas expressed by the owner and the architect. And, they must convey the spirit of the work.

Working drawings should be done in an economical, efficient manner. Fees are generally limited; expenses are significant. Architects who practice as a means of livelihood will need to hold a healthy balance between the two.

My purpose is to describe a process for preparing working drawings. My intent is to make the scope of this work clear, to encourage the formation of an orderly sequence of events, and to provide an aid for thorough completion of the job.

INTRODUCTION

Skim through the pages to see how the Handbook is organized. Designed for reference use, it will easily fit on a drafting board. The type has been set so that the body of the text is to the left, allowing a generous margin on the right for the reader's own notes.

There are four parts. Part One discusses drafting standards, time budgeting, and drawing layouts. Part Two presents the process and gives a description, example, and check list for each element in the set of working drawings. Part Three explains how to use more than one person in the drafting process, covers reproduction of drafting and project planning, shows how to estimate drafting costs, and covers changes and revisions. Part Four describes a way to coordinate, check, and complete the work.

Once familiar with the design and layout, study the text to grasp the philosophy behind the process. Visualize what each element is designed to communicate and how workmen will respond to them.

The handbook should be used as a guide and a tool. Keep it open and handy as you proceed through a set of drawings in a step by step fashion. Use the checklists both to assure completion of each element as you proceed and to assure the coordination and checking of each set at the end of the process.

As you develop your own ideas while working along, make notes in the margins at the right of each page. If you find a better way, revise it and rearrange it; let the handbook evolve into your own. Let it describe your personal process for producing a set of working drawings.

CONTENTS

PART ONE

Standards should be adopted prior to beginning a set of working drawings. While drawings themselves are a creative expression, standards help unify the set into a whole. They also eliminate petty decision making and allow the draftsman to apply his creative energy to the building design. Standards will facilitate cross referencing and retrieval of information from the drawings.

The most obvious standard is the title block on each sheet, which identifies the work with a particular design firm. Parties having an interest in the project will refer to the title block when making contact with the designers. It should include the logo, the name, the address, and the phone number of the firm. There should be room for job titles, sheet numbers and professional seals. The date is also an essential part of a title block.

Job titles fit into the title block and serve to identify each sheet as a portion of the contract documents. For this reason, each job title should be exactly the same, and should include name, number, street address, and locale. Office personnel use this information for filing, while supply companies use it for deliveries.

The various elements, or individual drawings which make up the set, should be titled for clear identification, relationship to scale, and cross reference to other elements.

NOTES

Section cuts, detail cuts, and north arrows also should be standardized. This will allow for quick, easy location and cross reference to the drawn elements.

The appearance of drawings can be further enhanced by the use of standardized lettering. This becomes important when more than one person works on the drawings. Although it is not practical for individuals to letter precisely the same, it is possible to adopt a similar style, size and spacing.

Standards naturally depend upon the cooperation of all members of a team. Utilization of such standards will save drafting time and will unify the appearance of drawings.

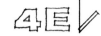

4E

SECTION MARK FOR CROSS
SECTIONS OR DETAILS

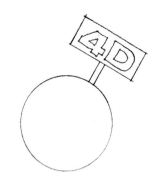

DETAIL REFERENCE

N

NORTH ARROW

ABCDEFGHIJKLMNOPQRSTUVWXYZ 123456789
123456789 ABCDEFGHIJKLMNOPQRSTUVWXYZ $10'-9\frac{1}{2}''$ ⌶ $\frac{1}{4} \times 4 \times 0'-7''$ ℄

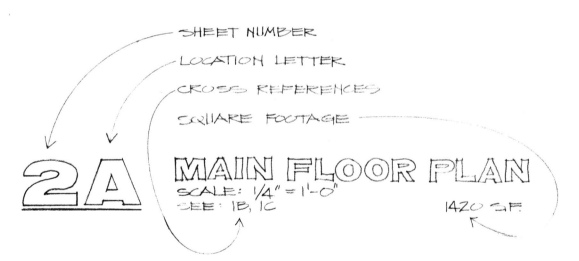

SHEET NUMBER
LOCATION LETTER
CROSS REFERENCES
SQUARE FOOTAGE

2A MAIN FLOOR PLAN
SCALE: 1/4" = 1'-0"
SEE: 1B, 1C   1420 S.F.

STANDARDS

Another initial consideration is the preparation of a time budget. This is needed to clarify the number of hours, days, or weeks which can be spent on the project. The fee and office expenses are the primary factors that affect a time budget.

Budgetaly influences will vary from office to office and from job to job. When an American Institute of Architects (A.I.A.) contract form is used, the fee breaks down this way:

Schematic Design	15%
Design Development	20%
Working Drawings	40%
Contract Negotiations	5%
Observation	20%

These figures show that 40% of the fee can be allocated to the working drawings. From the budget figures, subtract all relative expenses, such as consultant fees and printing costs. The result, when divided by an hourly billing rate, yields the time budget.

This is best shown by working through the following hypothetical example.

Fee		$6,000.00
Working Drawings	40%	2,400.00
Expenses	(−)	100.00
Drafting Budget	=	2,300.00
Hourly Rate	+	$10.00/hour
Time Budget	=	230 hours
		or 5¾ weeks

A means of control is needed if the time budget is to be of value. This can be done with a production graph, which plots time spent against percentage of completion. One plot on the graph is hypothetical, based on the average percentage table on the next page. The accompanying plot is based on actual time spent. By comparing the actual line with the budgeted line, a reasonable tab can be kept on work in progress.

A budget, like any other plan, is no better than one's ability to adhere to it. By staying as close to the budget line as possible, work should proceed in an orderly manner and should be completed in the time allowed.

AVERAGE PERCENTAGE TABLE

ELEMENT	% TIME	% COMPLETION
Layout	2	2
Floor Plans	10	12
Schedules	3	15
Site Plan	5	20
Structural	13 ⎫	33
Foundation	3 ⎬ 21 %	36
Framing	5 ⎭	41
Sections	10	51
Elevations	8	59
Electrical (Utilities)	2	61
Window Details	5	66
Dimensions	8	74
Interior Elevations	3	77
Miscellaneous	3	80
Specifications	3	83
Check	17	100

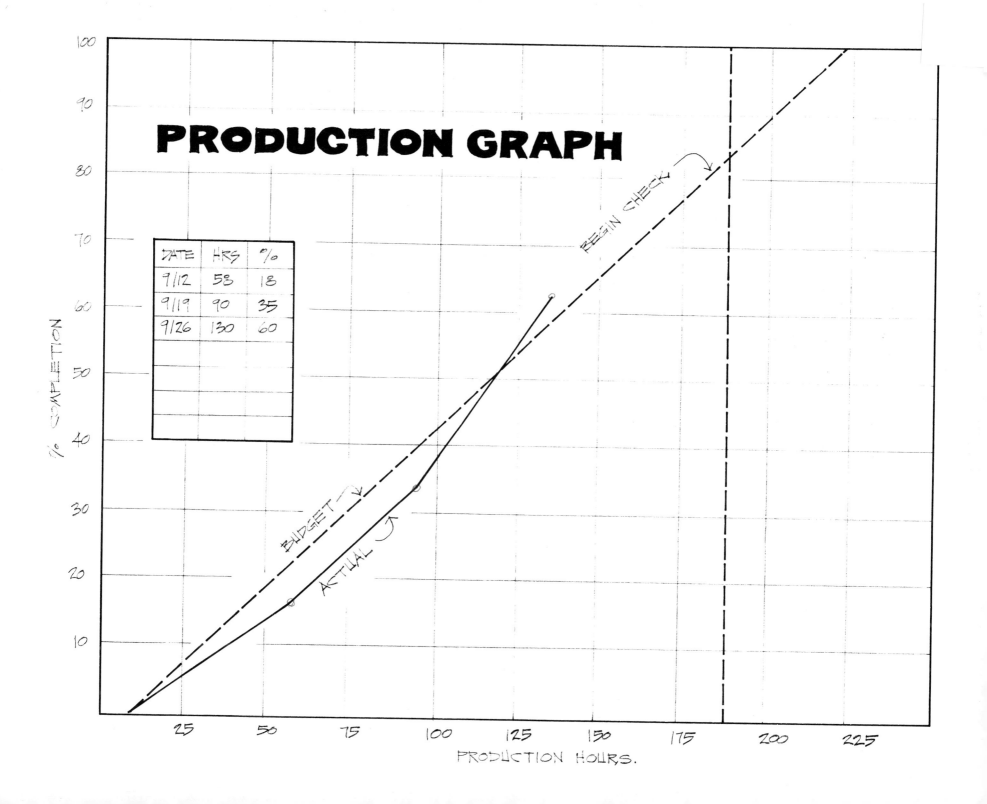

PRODUCTION GRAPH

DATE	HRS	%
9/12	58	18
9/19	90	35
9/26	130	60

% COMPLETION

PRODUCTION HOURS.

BEGIN CHECK

BUDGET

ACTUAL

Begin working drawings by laying out the entire set. This will allow perception of the drawings as a whole before each element is drawn in detail.

Select the number of sheets first and apply the margins and title blocks. All title information should be filled in at this time to assure that preliminary prints with partial information will be positively identified, that all title blocks will read precisely the same, and that this task will not have to be hastily done at the end of the job.

Then assign each element of the drawings to a specific page by notations in light pencil at one corner of each sheet. Elements which relate to one another should be located in close proximity so workmen in the field can easily extract the information they need. A layout guide at the end of this chapter is provided for assistance.
Next, the individual sheets are layed out by drawing in outlines of the assigned elements. Title guide lines and proposed dimension lines may also be penciled in at this time.

Adjustments will have to be made before each sheet is designed to satisfaction. Such work should be sketched in lightly in pencil. It may appear to be time wasted at first, but it is far less time-consuming than erasing and moving completely drawn elements.

After each sheet is designed, review the entire set with the layout guide, making sure that all the required elements are included in the set.

FIRST SHEET	SCALE
Site Plan	1″ = 20.0′ or 30.0′
Site Profile	1″ = 20.0′ or 30.0′
Soils Data	
Foundation Plan	⅛″ or ¼″ = 1′
Foundation Details	½″ = 1′
Landscaping Details	¾″ = 1′
Material Legend	
Sheet Index	

SECOND SHEET	
Floor Plans	⅛″ or ¼″ = 1′
Room Schedule	
Door Types	¼″ = 1′
Door Frames	1″ or 1½″ = 1′
Room Elevations	¼″ = 1′
Framing Plans	⅛″ or ¼″ = 1′

LAYOUT GUIDE

11

THIRD SHEET

Elevations	⅛″ or ¼″ = 1′
Window Details	1″ or 1½″ = 1′
Window Schedule	
Exterior Details	1″ or 1½″ = 1′

FOURTH SHEET

Cross Sections	¼″ or ⅜″ = 1′
Wall Sections	⅜″ or ½″ = 1′
Stair Section	⅜″ or ½″ = 1′
Handrailing Details	1″ or 1½″ = 1′
Fireplace Detail	⅜″ or ½″ = 1′
Structural Details	½″ or ¾″ = 1′
Miscellaneous Details	1″ or 1½″ = 1′

FIFTH SHEET

Electrical Plans	⅛″ or ¼″ = 1′
Heat Layout	⅛″ or ¼″ = 1′
Fixture Schedule	
Symbol Legend	

PART TWO

A process may be described as a natural sequence of events which leads to a favorable result. When a process is followed, solutions are discovered in a smooth, flexible, and efficient manner.

Buildings are designed through process, from schematics, to design development, to working drawings, to construction. It is important to be aware that production of the working drawings plugs into this sequence at a specific point, and enhances the growth of the building design.

Schematic and design development drawings are more easily and less expensively revised than working drawings. Consequently, construction drawings must not be started too soon. The beginning of this phase should be initiated after all of the major design decisions have been settled. This handbook describes the particular process which begins at this point.

One cannot become more efficient on a drafting table by trying to draw faster. Time saving comes through awareness of the entire process and through knowledge of what to draw next.

The process described on the flow chart at the end of this chapter illustrates the flow of elements as the drawings take form. The steps have been placed in a particular order. The elements which are drawn first provide the information needed to execute the ones which follow. As a person works through the process, knowledge of the building grows in his mind, while its image takes shape on the paper.

Efficiency in working with the process is keyed to discipline. Each step should be taken as near to completion as possible before moving on to the next step. Back tracking should be minimized and minor details left for the check at the end.

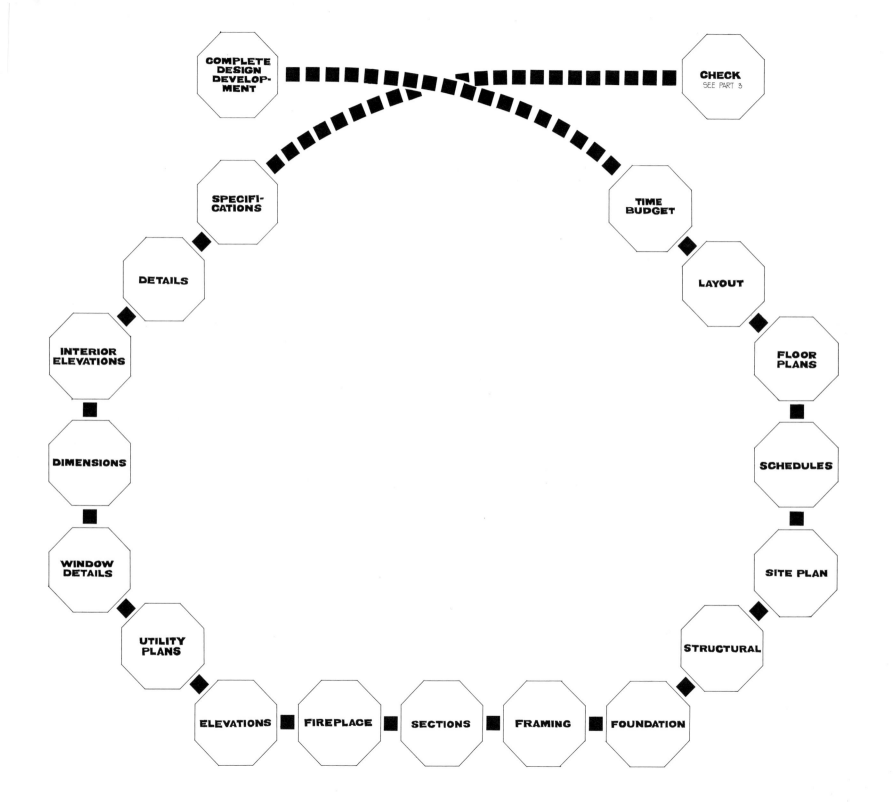

Floor plans are the most fundamental element in a set of working drawings. Each plan is a horizontal projection of the room layout for the floor it represents.

Many basic decisions are made while drawing the floor plans. Knowledge of the building is gained and recorded, and, as the plans are formulated, a matrix evolves for all the other key elements of the set.

Floor plans are also the most useful elements to the builder. They provide him with a basic reference point. He uses the plans to visualize, to estimate, and to lay out the work he will perform.

As much time will be spent on the floor plans as on any other element. This is because of the many questions which must be answered before the plans can be completed. In keeping with the spirit of process, the following sequence of events seems most logical: layout, walls, door swings, fixtures, cabinets, room names, schedule marks and poche.
Dimension lines with lettering guides follow up the drawing of the plans. No dimensions are done at this point, however, as they are a separate step in the process, as shown on the flow chart. They should be deferred until all the basic elements have been drawn and a more intimate knowledge of the building has been gained.

Before moving on to the next step, floor plans should be reviewed with the check list included in this chapter. A close check will assure that the plans have been taken as close to completion as possible.

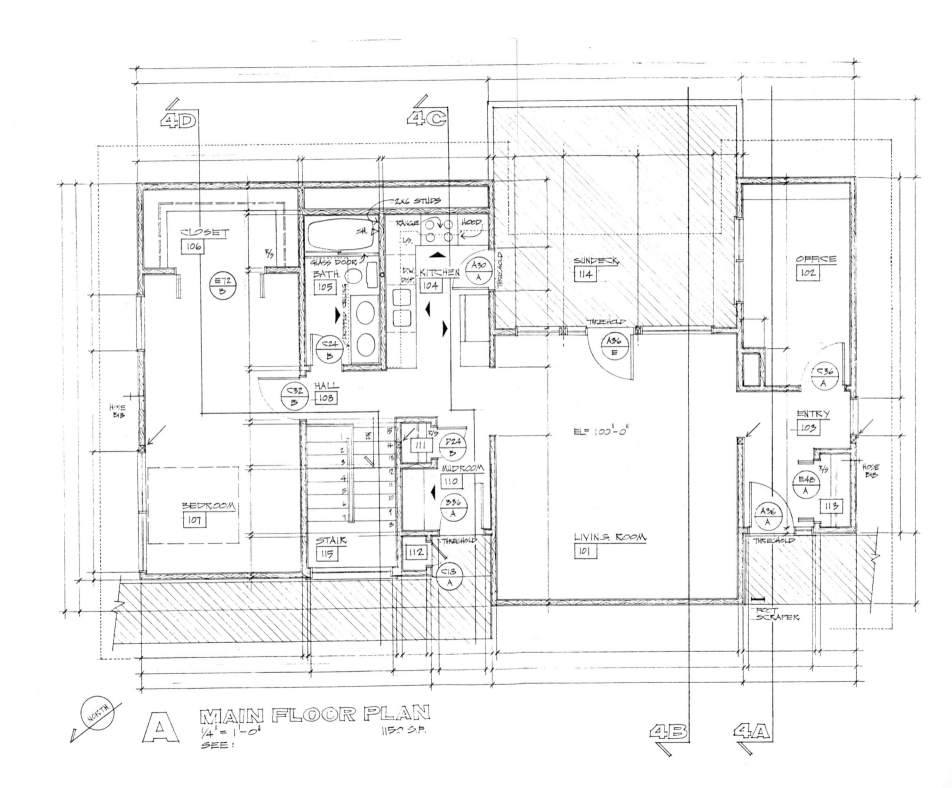

CLOSET
106

E72
B

BATH
105

SH.

GLASS DOOR

~2×6 STUDS

RANGE

HOOD

D.S.

D.W.
DISP.

KITCHEN
104

A30
A

THRESHOLD

SUNDECK
114

OFFICE
102

C24
B

C32
B

HALL
108

THRESHOLD

A36
E

C36
A

HOSE
BIB

BEDROOM
107

5
4
3
2
1

15
14
13
12
11
10
9
8

7
6
5
4
3
2
1

111

MUDROOM
110

D24
B

336
A

ELF 100'-0"

ENTRY
103

E48
A

113

HOSE
BIB

STAIR
115

112

THRESHOLD

C18
A

LIVING ROOM
101

A36
A

THRESHOLD

FOOT
SCRAPER

NORTH

A MAIN FLOOR PLAN
¼" = 1'-0"
SEE !

1150 S.F.

4D

4C

4B   4A

FLOOR PLAN CHECK LIST

Element title and number
Scale: ⅛″ or ¼″ = 1′.
Cross Reference Square Footage.
North Arrow.

Show all walls, partitions, and openings.
Identify all material in plan.
Show all structural posts and columns.

Windows

Show all windows and fixed glass.

Check operator location in reference to desired ventilation.

Doors

Swings shown—make sure they don't conflict.

Reference numbers.

Thresholds noted on exterior doors.

Show indication of frame.

Side lights occur at side knob of door.

Storm and screen doors called out.

Make sure there is room and shelf for muddy shoes by exterior doors.

Kitchen Layout

Show separate @ ¼″ if complex—verify with plan.

Refrigerator, dishwasher, disposal, range hood, lazy susan, trash masher, broom closet, ice maker.

Elevation marks to show wall elevations of all cabinets.

Cabinets dotted where above.

Work space between sink and stove.

Verify layout with catalog cabinet sizes.

Dash in kitchen table.

Bathroom Layout

Check line of site through door.

No door opening directly on area of food service or preparation.

Toilet, shower, shower rod or glass door, tub, vanity, and partitions.

Elevation marks to show wall elevations where mill work occurs.

Extra thick wall for plumbing behind toilet.

Check to see that water closet and bathtub traps miss framing.

Check all piping and waste traps to insure against frost.

Check route of stack vent or vent stack through roof.

Bedroom Layout

Include closet with rod and shelf with 2'-0" minimum overall depth.

Check furniture layout with respect to circulation and ventilation.

Locate bed with dashed line.

Stairs

Show all steps with riser numbers.

Show all railings.

Show up/down arrows.

Check stair width, rise, and run for compliance with code.

Show all steps in concrete.

Step beyond exterior door.

Check circular stair width for furniture access.

Mechanical

Locate furnace or boiler.

All plumbing fixtures shown and key to schedule.

Show all exterior freeze-proof hose bibs.

Locate all stacks and roof drains.

Check sound control on all stacks.

Review all heating elements, air diffusers, and return air grilles with furniture and drapery layout.

Dryer vent noted.

Floor drain where lower floor is a concrete slab.

Dimensions

Show all dimension lines with guide lines for lettering in the numbers. Hold off on the numbers until all major elements are drawn.

Overall dimensions to top and to the left.

To all breaks in wall.

To all windows and openings.

To all structural items.

To all partitions.

Elevation of floor levels noted.

Wall thickness.

Balcony dimensions—verify with roof overhang.

Fireplace hearth.

Stairs dimensionally located.

Miscellaneous

Show all section and detail cuts.

Identify all spaces.

  Room designation.

  Number.

Show roof overhang dotted above.

Overlay all floor plans with each other, structural and mechanical, to be sure all items line up and/or allow passage as required.

Note all dropped ceiling locations.

Show provision for trash storage.

Show walks and exterior amenities immediately adjacent to building.

Foot scraper and grate or recessed link mat. Note location of details.

Fire extinguisher location.

Guard rails at all area wells, openings, and stairs to protect people from falling in.

Door closer required on door from garage to interior of house.

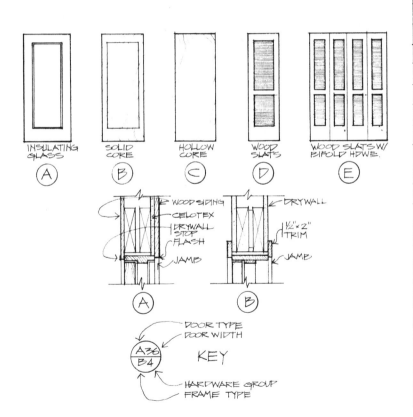

B DOOR TYPES

A	B	C	D	E
INSULATING GLASS	SOLID CORE	HOLLOW CORE	WOOD SLATS	WOOD SLATS W/ BIFOLD HDWE.

Detail A:
- WOOD SIDING
- CELOTEX
- DRYWALL STOP
- FLASH
- JAMB

Detail B:
- DRYWALL
- 1½" x 2" TRIM
- JAMB

KEY
- DOOR TYPE
- DOOR WIDTH
- A36 / B4
- HARDWARE GROUP
- FRAME TYPE

C ROOM FINISH SCHEDULE

Legend: ⊠ FINISH ON WALL SHOWN ONLY   ☐● FINISH ON ALL WALLS

Nº	NAME	Troweled Concrete	Carpet	Asphalt Tile	Wood Decking	Other	Wood	4" Resilient Cove	Ceramic Tile	½" Gypsum Board	Wood Siding as noted in Remarks	Ceramic Tile	Masonry	Masonite Pegboard	½" Gypsum Board	T&G Pine Boards	REMARKS
101	LIV./DIN.		●				●				●				●		R.S. CEDAR E.W. WALLS CEILING BOARD H. WALL.
102	OFFICE		●				●				●				●		R.S. CEDAR E.N.W. WALLS CEILING BOARD S. WALL
103	ENTRY		●	●			●			●					●		BARN SIDING ON WALLS
104	KITCHEN			●				●		●					●		
105	BATH		●				●			●		●			●		WATER RESISTANT DRYWALL & CERAMIC IN TUB
106	CLOSET		●				●			●					●		PROVIDE ROD & SHELF
107	BEDROOM		●				●			●					●		
108	HALL		●				●			●					●		BARN SIDING ON CLOSET
109	TRASH	●											●		●		
110	MUD ROOM		●	●			●			●					●		
111	CLOSET		●				●			●					●		PROVIDE ROD & SHELF
112	SKI ROOM				●		●				●				●		MATCH EXTERIOR SIDING PROVIDE SKI RACK
113	CLOSET			●			●								●		PROVIDE ROD & SHELF
114	SUNDECK				●												
115	STAIR		●				●			●					●		WOOD RAILING
201	HALL		●				●			●					●		
202	BATH		●				●			●		●			●		WATER RESISTANT DRYWALL & CERAMIC IN TUB
203	BEDROOM		●				●			●					●		
204	BEDROOM		●				●			●					●		
205	LAUNDRY			●				●		●					●		PROVIDE 2 SHELVES OVER MACHINES
206	LAVATORY			●				●		●					●		
207	BAR			●				●		●					●		
208	LINEN			●	●		●			●					●		
209	MECHANICAL	●								●					●		

Many materials which become part of a building are not integral to its structure. Yet, the construction of the building is affected by their use. These products come in different forms, are standardized, and have a variety of sizes. Items of the same category are interchangeable within the building.

This allows many options for the architect and his clients. Selections are made for the different materials to be used. These are then passed on to the builder.

Schedules are graphic aids to communication which convey this kind of information. They are keyed to the basic elements of the working drawings and are located close to the relating element.

Scheduling of room finishes, doors, and windows should be done at this time. This creates an opportunity for the draftsman to take a mental look at all the space and openings within a building. As decisions are made and recorded, a mental image begins to grow in his mind. Much information is stored for later use, such as opening sizes gained by scheduling the doors and windows.

The same benefit can be gained by reviewing schedules. This should be a first step for any person plugging into the process at any point.

Schedules should be simple, clear, and easily read. They must be specific. They must communicate. They must be easily changed. They must be keyed to the drawings. Many forms of schedules are acceptable, as long as they satisfy these requirements.

SCHEDULES

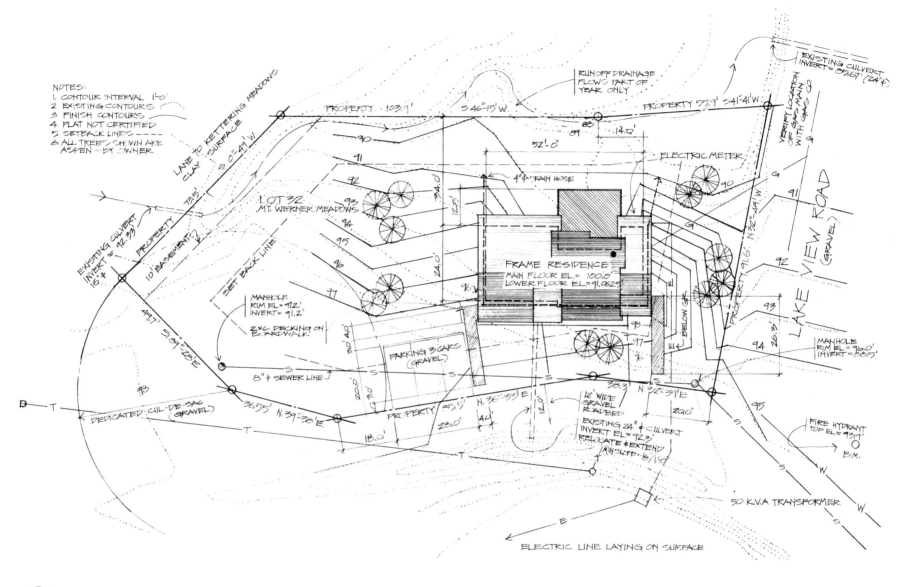

NOTES:
1. CONTOUR INTERVAL 1'-0"
2. EXISTING CONTOURS ———
3. FINISH CONTOURS
4. PLAT NOT CERTIFIED
5. SETBACK LINES ———
6. ALL TREES SHOWN ARE ASPEN - BY OWNER

RUN OFF DRAINAGE FLOWS PART OF YEAR ONLY

EXISTING CULVERT INVERT = 95.67' (24"ø)

PROPERTY 103.9'   S 46°-15' W.   PROPERTY 55.9' S 41°-41' W.

ELECTRIC METER

VERIFY LOCATION OF GAP MAIN WITH GAS CO.

LANE TO KETTERING MEADOWS CLAY SURFACE

S 0°-49' W

LAKE VIEW ROAD (GRAVEL)

4"ø DRAIN HOSE

LOT 32 MT. WERNER MEADOWS

10' EASEMENT

SET BACK LINE

FRAME RESIDENCE
MAIN FLOOR EL.= 100.0'
LOWER FLOOR EL.= 91.0625'

BELOW GR.

MANHOLE RIM EL = 97.2' INVERT = 91.2'

2×6 DECKING ON BOARDWALK

EXISTING CULVERT INVERT = 92.33'

PROPERTY

MANHOLE RIM EL.= 96.0' INVERT = 88.5'

PARKING 3 CARS (GRAVEL)

8"ø SEWER LINE

DEDICATED CUL-DE-SAC (GRAVEL)

N 39°-38' E

PROPERTY 95.5'   N 36°-37' E

12' WIDE GRAVEL ROADBED

EXISTING 24"ø CULVERT INVERT EL.= 92.3' RELOCATE & EXTEND (MIN. SLOPE 1/6 1/2)

FIRE HYDRANT TOP EL.= 93.9'
B.M.

50 K.V.A. TRANSFORMER

ELECTRIC LINE LAYING ON SURFACE

  NORTH **D** **SITE PLAN**
1" = 20'-0"
SEE;

An image of space forms in a draftsman's mind while the schedules are being completed. Now this image must be tailored to fit the lay of the land.

The site plan is a graphic representation of the contour of the ground in horizontal projection. It shows the location of the building and its amenities with respect to the land, and to the legal boundary around the land.

Knowledge and perception of the slope of the ground is gained by drawing the site plan. The draftsman will use this information to develop the elements which follow.

The site plan tells the builder where to find reference points and how to lay out the work. It also conveys the information he needs to estimate and execute the site construction required in his contract.

The site plan becomes a record to both the owner, and the municipality of the building location. For this reason, it needs to be explicit, exact, and complete. The check list which follows is provided to help achieve these qualities.

SITE PLAN CHECK LIST

Element Title and Number.
Scale: 1″ = 20.0 for house; 1″ = 30.0 large site.
Cross Reference.
North Arrow.
Designation of existing and finish grade.
Contour Interval.

Property Description

Property boundary.

    Identify each leg with word property.

    Bearing and distance of each leg.

    Corner description.

    Tie to section or ¼ corner.

Lot and block lines.

Building setback line.

Easements.

Brief legal description—lot number and subdivision or section and township.

Acreage or square footage.

Site Features and Topography

Contour lines.

2′-0″ maximum interval, 1′-0″ for flat terrain.

Bench mark—assumed or actual elevation.

Spot elevations.

Building corners.

Critical drainage points.

Walks and steps.

Curbs and gutters.

Sewer inverts.

Natural Features

Trees.

Rock outcroppings, ledge.

Springs, streams, ground water.

Name all streams and show direction of flow.

Drainage

Check minimum slope of all drainage 2% around building.

Check to see that drainage off property is directed to natural channels and will be similar to prior flow.

Check entire site by grid to see that flow is proper.

Foundation drain.

Slopes

Check maximum and minimum slopes for access and drainage—25% maximum, 2% minimum.

Check building form in relation to slope.

Check mass and slope in relation to human scale, both within and outside building.

Streets and Roads

Dimensions.

    Width of right of way.

    Snow removal easements and storage.

    Curve data.

    Bearings and distance.

    Corner radii.

Pavements

Description.

Extent.

Elevations.

Sidewalks and Curbs

Width.

Material.

Elevation.

Detail marks.

Names of Streets or Highways

Slopes

6% maximum for easy access.

2% for parking.

Bridges and Culverts

Dimensions of structure.

Size of openings.

Invert elevations.

Utilities

Water—Sewer—Gas.

    Location, dimension from property line or corner.

    Size and description of conduits.

    Invert elevations, depth of conduits below grade.

    Building drains, septic tanks, leaching fields.

    Wells and cisterns.

    Water pressure from main.

Electricity and Telephone

Verify entrances with utility company and provide space for their requirements.

If underground, previous section applies.

Locate all poles, transformers, and entrances with KVA, voltages noted.

Locate all outdoor lights.

Location dimension to lot line one corner.

Locate transformer.

Fire Hydrant

Size.

Location.

Elevation.

Storm Sewer and Foundation Drains

Invert elevation—check to see that water cannot back up into area drains or foundation drains.

Size and location.

Terminal point of roof drainage.

Improvements and New Buildings

Locate all structures existing and proposed.

Identify all buildings and note new construction.

Roof edge solid line, wall dashed line.

Overall dimensions and setbacks from two sides.

Main floor elevation, each building.

Existing building description.

Show roof drains and chimneys.

Elevations at building corners.

Check to see that entire building is located within the property line and setback line.

Rooftop units and other items on roof.

Walks, Drives, Patios, and Parking

Amenities and Existing Items

Show all existing items to be demolished and removed by contractor.

Landscaping Items

Locate and call out new trees and plants.

Check relation of all planting to human scale and activity.

Show extent of grass turf, planted grass, and/or other surface cover.

Other

Soil test hole location.

Draw profile through site at locations which best define the relationship of the building to site.

Special note where plan is not accurate: "Site plan taken from uncertified plat, verification required by contractor before construction begins."

Special note where trench required near power cable or gas. "Caution—electric/gas line to be located and protected. Contractor verify location with utility company prior to digging."

Structural calculations are a means of obtaining the information needed to draw the framing plans, foundation plans, and connection details. They are not part of the working drawings, but they become part of the architect's records. The calculations may be needed later to check the work, to execute structural revisions, or to verify competence in liability claims against the architect.

The primary purpose of the calculations is to assure the owner and the architect of a safe, sound, and serviceable structure. While doing them, the designer gains an intimate knowledge of what holds the building together, and determines what the structural member sizes will be.

Structural design is the reverse of the building process. It starts at the roof and works it's way down to the foundation, transferring loads as it progresses down. The beginning step is to sketch out the frame, paying particular attention to load transfer points. Then, each member is designed, from the top of the building to the bottom, using the check iists as a guide.

Consultants are used for this work where projects are large and sophisticated. When this is the case, a draftsman must pay particular attention to the information transmitted to him from the structural designer. However the structure is designed, the draftsman must know the member sizes, and how they fit together to form the skeleton of the building.

STRUCTURAL CALCULATIONS CHECK LIST

Index of Calculations

Design Data Record

Job title and job number.

Location of structure.

Building codes and manuals used.

    General.

    Steel.

    Wood.

    Concrete.

    Snow load data.

Type construction.

    UBC, type.

    General description.

Unit stresses.

    Steel.

    Concrete.

    Wood.

Soil data.

    Record of soil consultant with report date and job number.

STRUCTURAL

NOTES

Type soil.

Design values used.

Record of Complete Check with Building Code

Load Sheet

Dead loads.

Live loads.

Lateral loads.

Roof and floor totals.

Record of reductions taken.

Roof Design

Verify each calculation dimension with those on plans.

Decking and slabs.

Joists.

Beams, girders, trusses.

    Dead weight of member included.

    Area, section, moment of inertia and bearing.

Check all beams and cantilevers for,

    Worst possible condition of unbalanced load;

    Uplift on inside end;

    Possible locations for ice buildup and ponding.

36

Floor Design

Verify each calculation dimension with those on plans.

Decking and slabs.

Joists.

Beams, girders, trusses.

  Dead weight of member included.

  Consider live load reduction.

  Area, section, moment of inertia and bearing.

Review all long spans for deflections which could cause a drumming effect.

Check for worst possible condition of unbalanced loading.

Stair Design

Verify loading with building code.

Check all connections.

Load Rundown

Consider all columns and foundation conditions.

Consider all live load reductions.

NOTES

Walls

Check codes for maximum heights.

Check walls in bending for wind loading.

Design all wall columns for lateral loads.

Check minimum reinforcing of concrete and masonry walls.

Lintels

Check to see that all lintels have been designed.

Column Design

Refer to load rundown and see that all reductions have been taken.

Design cap and base plates.

Check code for minimum size and reinforcing of concrete columns.

Connections

Check to see that all connections are designed.

Check to see that all connections are compatible with finish materials and architectural details.

Foundation Design

Refer to soil report to be certain that correct design criteria have been used.

Dead load of spread footings included.

Grade beams.

    Dead load included.

    Deep beam formula.

    Check 10' soft spot.

Caisson design.

    Minimum reinforcing.

    End bearing.

    Surface friction.

Isolated column footings.

    Punching shear and normal shear.

    Moment design.

    Bond.

Fireplace support.

    Use fireplace formula, (2/3 volume × weight of materials).

    Consider differential settlements.

NOTES

Lateral pressures.

Verify that backfill materials specified are consistent with lateral design loads.

Check minimum reinforcing.

Retaining wall design.

Foundation = 0.06 #/ft, retaining wall = 0.03 #/ft unless soils engineer specifies.

Wind Analysis and Lateral Loads

Check walls for bending.

Run loads down to diaphragms and shear walls.

Design diaphragms and bracing.

Check all bracing connections.

Check uplift of shear walls.

Check diaphragm to shear wall connection.

Check building for earthquake loads.

U.B.C. or P.C.A. methods small buildings.

Check all diaphragms and shear wall connections.

Check x bracing connections.

Coordinate Specifications and Notes

Refer to specifications, foundation notes, and framing notes to see that all items are covered and that design criteria agree.

Complete Check

Check to see that each calculation has been reviewed for correctness and completeness.

Check each calculation for correct span and conditions shown on final drawings.

Miscellaneous

Check for possible locations where differential settlements and shrinkage might occur and provide a means to compensate for stresses.

Thoroughly check all calculations where design assumptions are liberal.

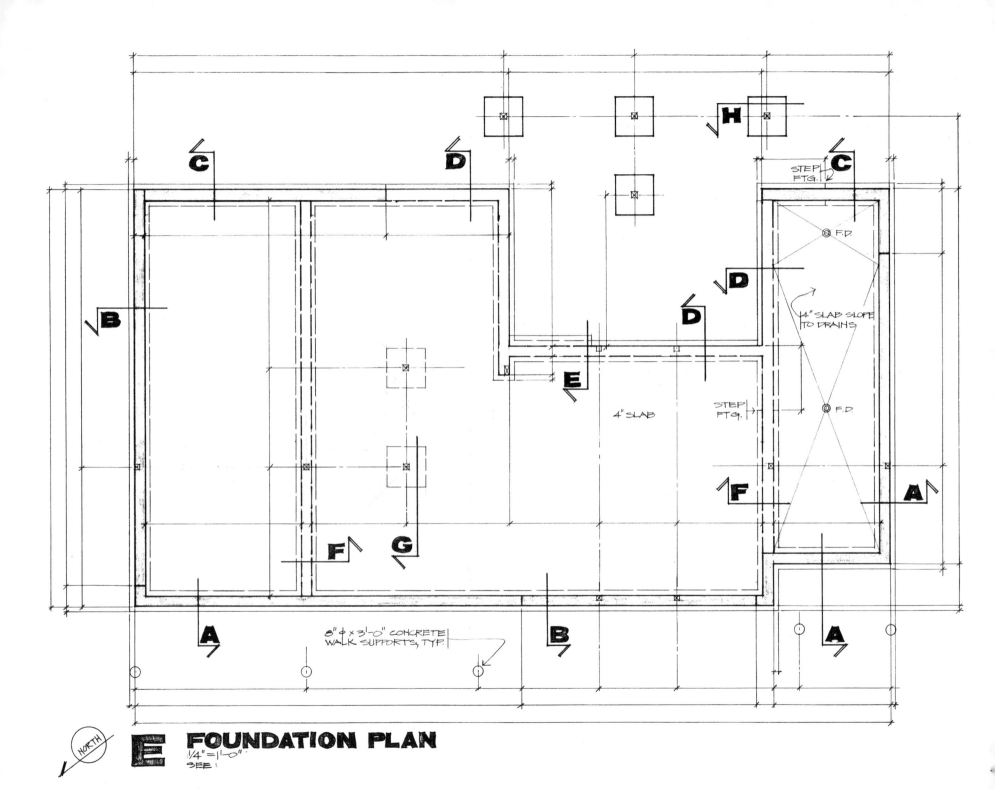

STEP
FTG.

4" SLAB SLOPE
TO DRAINS

F.D.

F.D.

4" SLAB

STEP
FTG.

8"φ x 3'-0" CONCRETE
WALK SUPPORTS, TYP.

NORTH

E FOUNDATION PLAN
1/4" = 1'-0"
SEE :

Foundation drawings include a plan view and sectional details for each different configuration.

The foundation fits naturally into the working drawing process at this point. Floor plan drawings have revealed the building layout. The land slope has been studied while doing the site plan. Load bearing points have been identified during the structural design. Now the draftsman can start to assemble the building on paper, and in his mind, starting from the foundation and working up.

The builder will use the foundation drawings to estimate labor and materials relative to the foundation work. He will be concerned with factors relating to temporary forms as well as factors relating to the permanent structure. His second interest in the drawings will be to extract the information he needs to lay out the work for actual construction.

Foundation drawings are simple and straightforward, showing only information relative to this work. Dimension lines are drawn but left blank for the same reason given with the floor plan description. A check list is provided here to help the draftsman include all the necessary items before proceeding on to the next step.

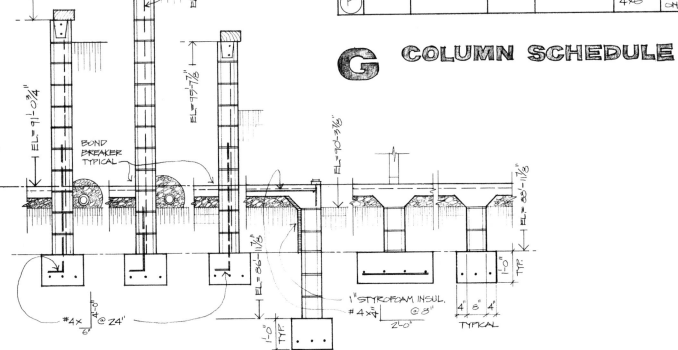

MK	2ND FLOOR	CONNECTION	1ST FLOOR	CONNECTION	BSMT.	CONNECTION	FDN.	CONNECTION	LOAD#
A			6×6	SIMPSON CC66	CONC.				14788
B			6×6	SIMPSON CC66	6×6 COL.				19437
C			6×8		CONC.				27649
D	5-2×4		6×6		6×6	SIMPSON BC6 ON BOTTOM			21004
E	6×6		6×6		CONC.				14470
F			3-2×4		6×6				16200
G			5-2×4		CONC.				10288
H			6-2×4		CONC.				14560
K			3-2×4		DOUBLE JOIST				
L			3-2×4		DOUBLE JOIST				
M			3-2×4		CONC.				12910
N					4×6	SIMPSON CC64 ON TOP			17890
P					4×6	SIMPSON CC64 ON TOP			5456

Ⓖ **COLUMN SCHEDULE**

CREOSOTED PLATE TYP.

DUR-O-WAL TYP. REINF.

EL=96'-3⅞"

EL=98'-11⅛"

EL=91'-0¾"

EL=95'-7⅛"

BOND BREAKER TYPICAL

EL=90'-3⅞"

EL=86'-11⅞"

EL=85'-11⅞"

#4× 4'-0"/6" @ 24"

1" STYROFOAM INSUL.
#4×4"

1'-0" TYP.

4" 8" 4"
2'-0"

4" 4"
TYPICAL

1'-0" TYP.

Ⓕ **FOUNDATION DETAILS**

½"=1'-0"

FOUNDATION CHECK LIST

Element Title and Number.
Scale: ⅛″ or ¼″ = 1′.
Cross Reference.
North Arrow.

Draw walls in plan showing all steps, caissons, and footings to scale. Show footing lines solid below fill, dashed below a concrete slab.

Standard Notes Below Title

All footings to bear on undisturbed materials regardless of elevations shown.

Description of floor slab.

Thickness.

Underlayment.

Welded fabric 6 × 6 10/10 lapped one full mesh and wired together at 4′-0″ o.c., or ⅜″ bars at 2′-0″ o.c.

Expansion strip.

Waterproofing.

Top of slab elevation.

Typical Footing Description

Width.

Thickness.

Re-bar and dowels.

Top el.̄ noted thus, (＿＿＿＿).

Typical Pad and Fireplace Footing

Width × length.

Thickness.

Reinforcing dowels.

Anchor bolts.

Top el.̄ noted thus, (＿＿＿＿).

Typical Caisson Description

Diameter.

Penetration to bedrock.

Minimum reinforcing.

Top el.̄ noted thus, (＿＿＿＿).

Typical Foundation Wall Description

Material.

Horizontal and vertical reinforcing.

Minimum and special reinforcing for masonry, grouted solid, bar lap noted and located.

All splices to be 36 (24) bar diameters.

Provide 18″ corner bars to match horizontal steel.

Bond beam.

Thickened Slab Note

Required below all masonry and bearing walls.

Refer to location of typical detail.

Anchor Bolt Note

Provide ⅝″ × 10″ anchor bolts at 32″ where wood framing joins concrete or masonry. Attach treated wood plate top of wall with ½″ @ 6′-0″ per code.

Dowel Note

Provide #4 × 6 × 1′-0″ dowels in slab at point where it bears on wall.

Embeco Grout Note

Provide embeco grout at all beam bearing and column bearing points.

Backfill Note

Contractor responsible for operation.

Temporary bracing required before framing installed.

Only approved materials used.

NOTES

Contractor responsible for drain tile, test after backfilling.

Drain Hose Note

Below Slab Insulation

Access to Crawl Space and Ventilation Openings

Waterproofing Note

Check to See that All Parts Are Shown

All walls solid line.

Footings—solid line below fill, dashed below concrete slab.

Thickened slab dashed line.

Draw × through slabs at same elevation.

Show steps in slab with dimension.
Show floor drain location and call out.

Show all columns and call out, include cap and base plate.

Show and note all beam pockets and inserts.

Note footing step and top of wall step elevations.

Show brick ledge or masonry angles.

Call out *treated* plate for wood frame.

Dimensions

Show all dimension lines with guide lines for lettering in the numbers. Hold off on the numbers until all major elements are drawn.

Overall dimensions to the top and to the left.

Add footing dimension at each end of overall dimension.

To all breaks in wall.

Caisson or pad footing layout.

To edge of all openings.

To all bearing walls, columns, thickened slabs, and isolated pads.

Wall thicknesses and footing extensions.

To all steps in walls and footing.

Show All Detail Cuts

One cut at each point where detail changes.

Foundation Details @ ½″ = 1′-0″

Draw one detail for each different condition.

Line up details such that elevations coincide.

NOTES

Show all reinforcing.

Top and bottom bars.

Footing bars.

Dowels.

Show anchor bolts and wood plate.

Show insulation below slab.

Show drain tile.

Show grade sloping away from building.

Slab with W.W.F. and gravel below.

Expansion joint or bond breaker.

Frost detail below door.

Thickened slab.

Post connections.

Poche all parts per material legend.

Miscellaneous Items

Check to see that bottom of foundation relates to existing grades.

No airpockets designed in.

Proper frost depth.

Check to see that top of foundation relates to finish grades.

Check to see than an insulated wall occurs at all frost lines.

Check to see that no exterior slab is detailed such that it will frost buckle doors, or settle with backfill.

Check to see that there is access and ventilation to crawl spaces.

Check all footing elevations with soil report.

Check to see that backfill note is on the drawings some place.

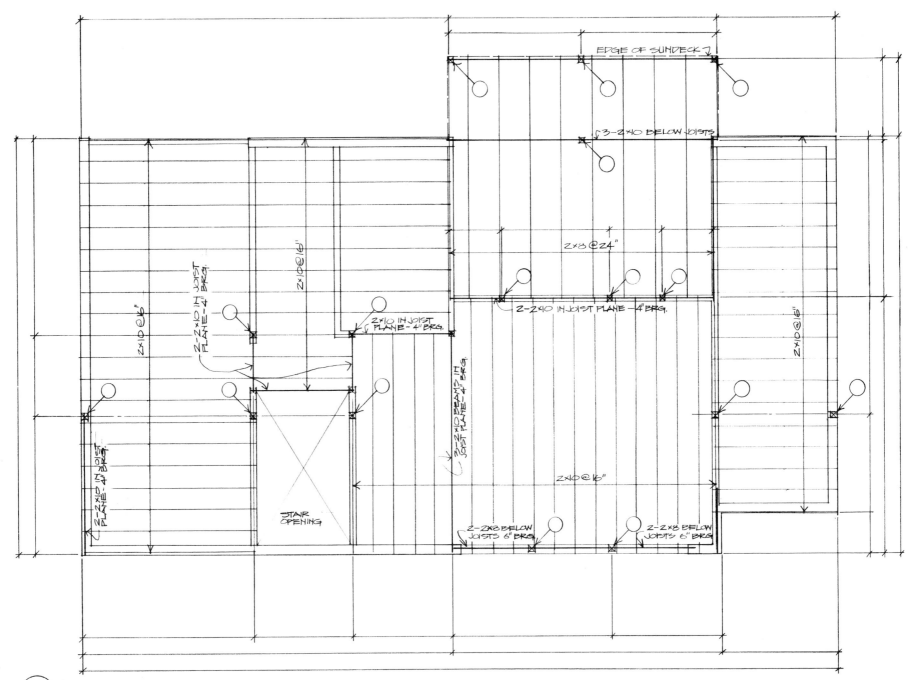

EDGE OF SUNDECK

3-2×10 BELOW JOISTS

2×8 @ 24"

2-2×10 IN JOIST PLANE - 4" BRG.

2×10 @ 16"

2×10 @ 16"

2×10 @ 16"

2-2×10 IN JOIST PLANE - 4" BRG.

2×10 IN JOIST PLANE - 4" BRG.

3-2×10 BEAM IN JOIST PLANE - 4" BRG.

2-2×10 IN JOIST PLANE - 4" BRG.

2-2×8 BELOW JOISTS 6" BRG.

2-2×8 BELOW JOISTS 6" BRG.

STAIR OPENING

NORTH

H FLOOR FRAMING PLAN
1/4"=1'-0"
SEE:

Framing plans are drawn floor by floor, starting at the lowest level and working up to the roof. Framing plans are horizontal projections of the building frame at each floor level and at the roof. Like floor plans, they are basic reference elements, with all connection details and sections keyed to them. The draftsman continues to build up his knowledge of the structure as he draws, here gaining knowledge of member sizes for use in drawing the sections.

The builder will refer to the framing plans to determine how to lay out the horizontal assemblies. This distinguishes them from the floor plans, which tell him how to lay out the vertical assemblies. The framing plans give him the data he needs to estimate costs, to order materials, and to lay out the work.

The framing plan check list provided will assist in the completion of these elements. Framing plans should be drawn with the principal in mind that they represent a horizontal section cut just above each floor. Columns extending above this floor to support upper levels should always be shown. Dimension lines are drawn but not filled in, as done with preceding elements.

FRAMING

FRAMING PLAN CHECK LIST

Element Title and Number.
Scale: ⅛″ or ¼″ = 1′.
Cross Reference.
North Arrow.

Draw frame in plan showing all bearing walls, beams, lintels, framing, and columns below plane of cut.

Notes Below Title

Live load used in design.

Typical decking and framing note.

  Type decking.

  Glue and nailing specified.

  Size and spacing of members.

  Top elevation of joists or bearing.

Typical bearing wall lintel.

Reference to typical connections required on all overhand joists and beams.

Bridging and blocking note, bridging at midspan, solid blocking at supports.

Embeco grout below beam bearing point.

Provide double joists or solid blocking @ 2′-0″ below all partitions.

Framing plans show structural requirements only. Additional members may be necessary for blocking, nailers, and code regulations.

Call Out All Structural Items Shown

Beams—designation of size, elevation and bearing.

Show columns and call out.

Joists—designation of size, elevation and spacing.

Stiffeners for steel beams.

Columns, caps, and base plates.

Connections.

Show All Detail Cuts

To describe all framing connections.

Where columns pass through floor.

All seat cuts for rafters.

Call Out Edge of Roof or Balcony

Note End of Cantilever Beams Extending Beyond Wall With "End Beam"

Note Slope of Roof by Arrow Pointing Down

NOTES

55

NOTES

Dimensions

Show all dimension lines with guide lines for lettering in the numbers. Hold off on the numbers until all elements are drawn.

Overall dimension to top and left of building.

To all bearing lines and columns.

To all openings requiring a beam.

To edge of all framing systems such that contractor can determine all member lengths.

To all beams such that contractor can determine lengths.

To center all beams for layout.

Bearing wall thicknesses.

Beam bearing lengths.

Overhang beams and joists.

Top of beam el.= where not obvious.

Miscellaneous Items

Check to see that all beams bear 6" to 8".

Check to see that standard framed rafters have a positive tie to ceiling.

Check to see that plumber can work around structure.

Toilet and bathtub traps.

Verify layout for all openings.

Ductwork and sky domes.

Check to see that all connections are covered.

Check through structural calculations to be sure everything is called out on the drawings.

Check over drawing and notes to be sure all lintels are covered.

Identify work points for dimensions if not obvious.

Check all roof drains to see that:

they fit within the framing;

that pipes will fit through interior partitions.

Check mechanical openings for strength.

Check to see that beams have proper bearing.

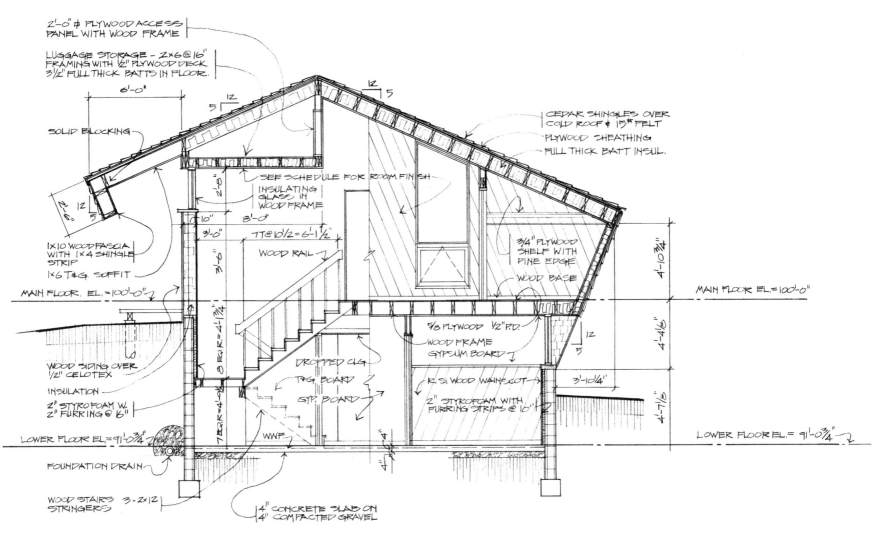

2'-0" ⌀ PLYWOOD ACCESS
PANEL WITH WOOD FRAME

LUGGAGE STORAGE - 2×6 @ 16"
FRAMING WITH ½" PLYWOOD DECK
3½" FULL THICK BATTS IN FLOOR.

6'-0"

SOLID BLOCKING

12   5

5   12

12   5

CEDAR SHINGLES OVER
COLD ROOF & 15# FELT
PLYWOOD SHEATHING
FULL THICK BATT INSUL.

SEE SCHEDULE FOR ROOM FINISH

INSULATING
GLASS IN
WOOD FRAME

2'-0"

1×10 WOOD FASCIA
WITH 1×4 SHINGLE
STRIP
1×6 T&G SOFFIT

10"

8'-0"

3'-0"

7T @ 10½ = 6'-1½"

WOOD RAIL

3'-6"

¾" PLYWOOD
SHELF WITH
PINE EDGE

WOOD BASE

4'-10¾"

MAIN FLOOR. EL.=100'-0"

MAIN FLOOR EL.=100'-0"

8 EQR = 4'-1¾"

5/8 PLYWOOD   ½" P.O.

WOOD FRAME
GYPSUM BOARD

12   5

4'-4⅛"

WOOD SIDING OVER
½" CELOTEX

DROPPED CLG.

T&G BOARD

R. S. WOOD WAINSCOT

3'-10¼"

INSULATION

GYP. BOARD

2" STYROFOAM W.
2" FURRING @ 16"

7 EQR = 4'-0¼"

2" STYROFOAM WITH
FURRING STRIPS @ 16"

4'-7⅛"

LOWER FLOOR EL.=91'-0¾"

WWF

4'-4"

LOWER FLOOR EL.= 91'-0¾"

FOUNDATION DRAIN

WOOD STAIRS 3-2×12
STRINGERS

4" CONCRETE SLAB ON
4" COMPACTED GRAVEL

J CROSS SECTION

¼"=1'-0"
SEE:.

All of the elements thus far have been projections in the horizontal plane. While these were being developed, a spatial conceptualization has been growing in the mind. This image will be expressed by drawing the sections.

Sections are projected views taken from vertical planes slicing through the building. They graphically describe the building in its third dimension. Wall sections are portions of sections usually drawn at a larger scale. They convey more detailed information and relate to the assembly of parts rather than the space. A stair section is a special condition which shows how to build the stairs.

The builder will find the sections to be as useful as the plans. After studying them, he will be able to visualize the space, and know how the structure ties together. He will also find information on applications such as insulation, flashing, and furring.

The information required on the sections is described in the check lists. There should be as many sections drawn as are needed to adequately describe the building. Each section should be complete, showing the contractor all the information he needs to estimate and to pursue his work.

CROSS SECTION CHECK LIST

Element Title, and Number.
Scale: ¼″ = 1′, ⅜″ = 1′, ½″ = 1′.
Cross Reference.

Show all walls, floors, beams, slabs, joists and blocking in section; all walls, cabinets, windows, and other architectural elements beyond in elevation.

Show all dimension lines with guide lines for lettering in the numbers. Show a heavy dot dash line at top of all floors, plates, beams, and stair landings with guide lines for lettering in the elevations. Hold off on the numbers until all the elements are drawn.

Elevations noted at:

Finish floors.

Plate lines.

Ridge beams.

All dimensions necessary for carpenters to lay out rafters, stairs, and walls.

Slab and gravel dimensions.

Dimensions to all interior railings.

All projections, overhangs, balconies, etc.

Chimney heights.

Sill and lintel heights.

Materials—show all materials in section and identify. Indicate size but do not specify quality as that is covered in the specifications. Where structural members are called out elsewhere, draw to scale only and provide reference note.

Poche materials in section as per material legend.

Note to see schedule for surface materials of wall elevation beyond.

Verify surface materials with room finish schedule.

Mechanical and Electrical

Show routing of plumbing vents by dashed line.

Show routing of roof drains by dashed lines and call out noise control.

Show routing of all ductwork and large piping.

Show all electrical fixtures and cross reference to schedule.

Show boiler and furnace flues.

Show vent for combustion air to boiler or furnace.

Enlarged Details—circle out areas which require clarification and for which details will be drawn.

Flashing for beams through walls.

Gravel stop if flat roof is used.

Paper under metal and folded over edge.

Asphalt and rock over metal.

NOTES

Frost detail below all doors.

Exterior slab moves without pushing door.

Styrofoam insulation inside below slab.

Insulation of slab from exterior cold temperatures.

Miscellaneous Items

Call out furring where concrete walls receive finish.

Show foundation drain.

Call out wind bracing at corners.

Vents required on soffit to prevent sweating.

Anchor bolts.

Expansion joints.

Voids below grade beams.

Detail of thickened slab.

Metal corners at mitred edges of plywood.

Slip joint detail at top of partitions where required because of expansive soil conditions.

Sealer below plate.

Provide pine edge nosing on edge of plywood tread.

Check to see that drip point on all overhangs extends past balcony railings.

Special Notes

Solid blocking is required for horizontal members at supports and cantilever ends; for vertical members at mid height; where necessary for vertical siding; and as backing for all cabinets, shelves, towel bars, soap dishes and miscellaneous hardware.

Note to slope grade away from building.

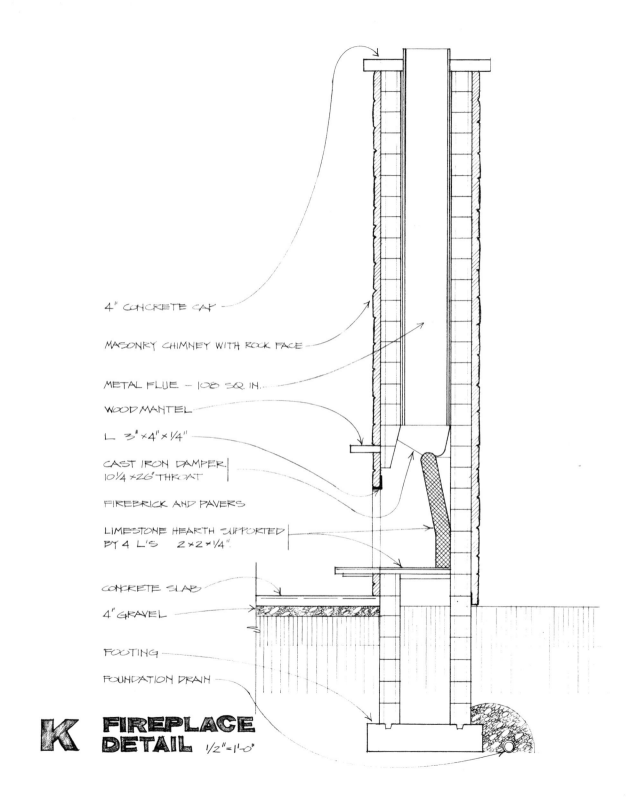

4" CONCRETE CAP

MASONRY CHIMNEY WITH ROCK FACE

METAL FLUE — 108 SQ. IN.

WOOD MANTEL

L 3" × 4" × 1/4"

CAST IRON DAMPER
10 1/4 × 26' THROAT

FIREBRICK AND PAVERS

LIMESTONE HEARTH SUPPORTED
BY 4 L'S   2 × 2 × 1/4".

CONCRETE SLAB

4" GRAVEL

FOOTING

FOUNDATION DRAIN

K FIREPLACE DETAIL 1/2" = 1'-0"

Fireplaces are described by use of a special wall section and an elevation of its front side. When practical, the fireplace drawings should be combined with another section.

The check lists describe the information needed on these drawings. Masons will use this information to estimate and to build the fireplace.

Fireplace drawings must be clear and easily read by the owner as well as the tradesmen. A fireplace is a very personal item in a home, one which the owner will closely identify with. The drawings must convey the spirit of the owner's desire to the tradesmen.

FIREPLACE

FIREPLACE DETAIL CHECK LIST

Element Title and Number.
Scale: ⅜″ or ½″ = 1′.
Cross Reference.

Verify Firebox—smoke chamber design with empirical formula.

Cross Section

Poche materials with as per material legend.

Show all fireplace parts and call out.

Ash dump—manufacturer and/or size.

Damper—manufacturer and/or size.

Firebrick or precast unit—manufacturer and/or size.

Smoke chamber.

Flue liner and/or size.

Call out opening size.

Steel angles supporting opening.

Hearth—call out reinforcing if concrete.

Screen.

Flashing.

Note all materials.

Show foundation and all related framing.

Elevation

Combine with building cross section or interior elevation if possible.

Show all flues with dashed line.

Show all facing materials and call out.

Show mantel and fire screen.

Dimensions

Vertical and horizontal dimensions.

Hearth dimensions 1'-6" minimum projection, 12" beyond opening on each end.

Flues

Check to see that all flues will fit.

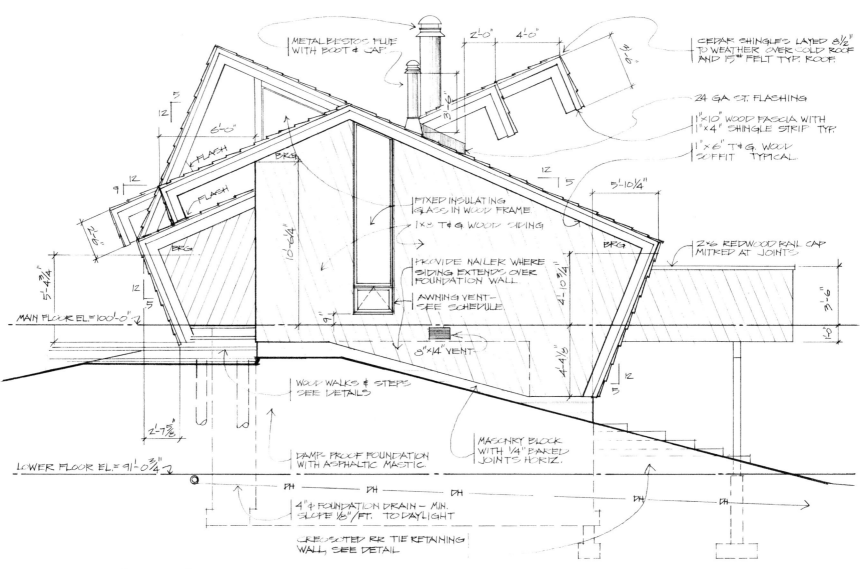

METAL BESTOS FLUE
WITH BOOT & CAP.

2'-0"   4'-0"

3'-6"

CEDAR SHINGLES LAYED 8½"
TO WEATHER OVER COLD ROOF
AND 15# FELT TYP. ROOF.

24 GA. ST. FLASHING

1"×10" WOOD FASCIA WITH
1"×4" SHINGLE STRIP TYP.

1"×6" T&G. WOOD
SOFFIT TYPICAL.

5   12

6'-0"

FLASH

9   12

FLASH

BRG

BRG

12   5

10'-6¼"

FIXED INSULATING
GLASS IN WOOD FRAME.

1×8 T&G. WOOD SIDING

12   5

5'-10¼"

BRG

2×6 REDWOOD RAIL CAP
MITRED AT JOINTS

5'-4¾"

PROVIDE NAILER WHERE
SIDING EXTENDS OVER
FOUNDATION WALL.

4'-10¾"

3'-6"

MAIN FLOOR EL.=100'-0"

AWNING VENT-
SEE SCHEDULE.

9"

4'-4⅛"

WOOD WALKS & STEPS
SEE DETAILS

8"×14" VENT

5   12

2'-7⅝"

DAMP-PROOF FOUNDATION
WITH ASPHALTIC MASTIC.

MASONRY BLOCK
WITH ¼" BAKED
JOINTS HORIZ.

LOWER FLOOR EL.= 91'-0¾"

DH   DH   DH   DH   DH

4"φ FOUNDATION DRAIN – MIN.
SLOPE ⅛"/FT. TO DAYLIGHT.

CREOSOTED RR TIE RETAINING
WALL, SEE DETAIL

 SOUTHWEST ELEVATION
¼"=1'-0"
SEE:

Elevations are vertical projections showing the exterior of the building from each side. They are a basic element, and a reference point for window details and exterior details.

The composition of the elevations has been known throughout the process. Their general arrangement was developed in the schematic and preliminary phases of design. With the space, structure, and site configurations now known, they can be precisely drawn to scale so that they fit the building and the site.

Elevations tell the builder how to enclose the structure. He will use them to estimate this work, and to guide him in its completion. The information which the elevations must convey is given in the check lists which follow.

ELEVATIONS

Elevations Check List

Element Title and Number.
Scale: ⅛″ or ¼″ = 1′
Cross Reference.

Show each side of building in projection to scale. Include dashed projection of foundation.

Notes

Show only on one elevation. Note that other elevations refer back to this one.

Identify all exterior materials but don't specify size or quality as this will be covered in the specifications.

Chimney materials.

Flashing.

Roof.

Fascia.

Soffit.

Windows.

Siding.

Foundation finish.

Damp proofing.

Gutters and leaders.

Balcony rail.

Beam caps.

Foundation vent.

Existing grade.

Dimensions

Show dimension lines with guide lines for lettering in the numbers. Show a heavy dot-dash line at the top of all floors, plates, and beams with guide lines for lettering in the elevation. Hold off on the numbers until all the elements are drawn.

Elevations noted at:

    Finish floors,

    Plate lines,

    Ridge beam.

Dimension all projections and cross check with floor and framing plans.

    Roof overhangs.

    Balconies.

    Beams.   Make sure drip point of roof overhang extends past balcony railing.

    Chimneys

Porch railings.

Call out all roof slopes and angle cuts on fascia.

NOTES

Windows

Check to see that all windows are shown in proper location to scale on both plan and elevation.

Key all operators to window schedule.

Dash lines to hinged edge.

Window detail cuts.

Check to see that no mullions are at eye level.

Glass decals noted in public space.

When glass is less than 18″ off floor, safety glass required.

Foundation

Refer to foundation plan and show with dashed line below grade.

Show all footing steps to scale.

Show foundation drain.

Check to see that entire footing is below grade.

Call out foundation ventilation and boiler vents.

Grades

Refer to site plan and show grade on elevation.

Show existing grade with dotted line on back, finish grade heavy solid line on front of sheet.

Check to see that grades relate at corners from one elevation to the next.

Porch, Balcony, and Stair Supports

Show posts, concrete pier, and footing.

Call out as typical note on one elevation.

Miscellaneous Items Shown and Noted

Splash blocks at hose bibs and down spouts.

Rain gutters and down spouts.

Drip diverters over steps and walks.

Foot scrapers.

Exterior lighting attached to building.

Show electric service and meter in detail; including transformer.

Show and call out all attic vents, foundation vents, mechanical fans, roof top units, and louvers.

Flashing required where level and reverse slope beams pass through to building.

Balcony rail details.

Fascia details and specify materials and back painting.

Cross Reference

Lay each elevation below side of plan which applies and check for correct projection.

Check to see that elevations of indentures and/or returns are covered.

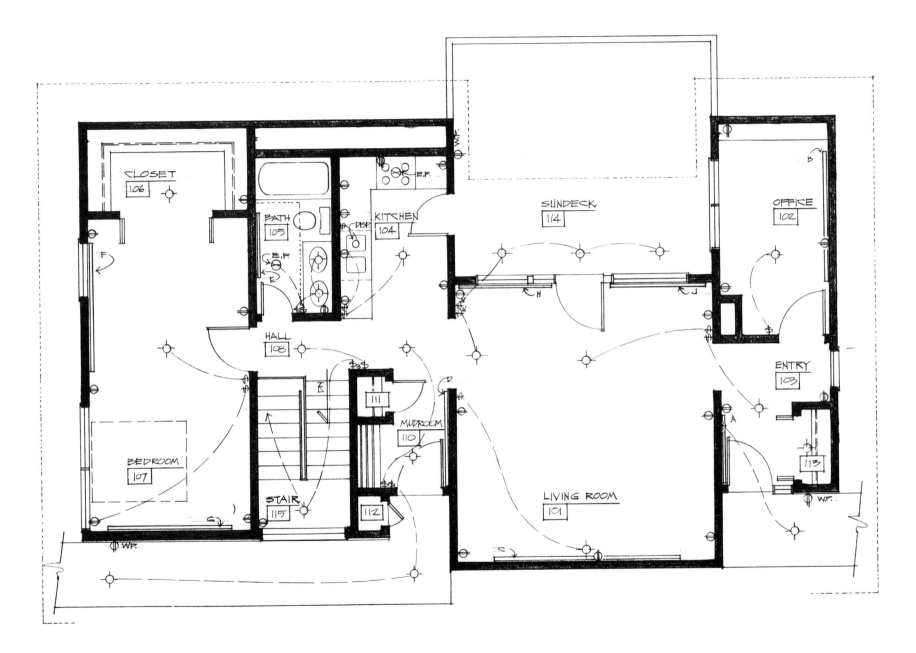

CLOSET
106

BATH
105

KITCHEN
104

E.F.

DISP.

E.F.

SUNDECK
114

OFFICE
102

B

HALL
108

H

J

$

ENTRY
103

BEDROOM
107

F

STAIR
115

111

MUDROOM
110

112

LIVING ROOM
101

A

113

W.P.

W.P.

S

W.P.

NORTH

UTILITY PLAN

1/4" = 1'-0"
SEE:

The form of the building has now been completely described. Attention in this step will focus on the items and equipment which make the spaces convenient and comfortable.

Utility plans convey this information to the builder and his subcontractors. Mechanical and electrical information is shown on these plans, which are similar to floor plans, with construction data and dimensions omitted.

The work described is traditionally done by subcontractors after the building frame has been assembled. To avoid confusing the different kinds of information, utility plans are drawn separately.

Most states require this work to be done by licensed tradesmen in accordance with provisions spelled out in codes. This eliminates the need for the draftsman to lay out each circuit and conduit.

Utility plans do require a specific description of the end results, done br drawing symbols on the plan for the items desired. The check list provided lists things which are needed. These should be shown in their exact location and drawn to scale.

UTILITY PLANS

Show Architectural Elements

Walls, windows, and openings.

Door and door swings.

Stairs.

Built in's and plumbing fixtures.

Room names and room numbers.

Locate All Electrical Convenience Items

Outlets, spaced at 12 feet.

Waterproofing outlets by exterior doors, balconies.

Outlets per code, kitchen and laundry.

Show height of outlet where not standard.

Lighting

All light fixtures.

All switches, accessible in logical location, not behind doors.

Key fixtures to schedule.

UTILITY CHECK LIST

Element Title and Number.
Scale: same as floor plan or ¼"
Cross Reference Square Footage.
North Arrow.

Show height on hanging and wall fixtures.

Outdoor light fixtures.

Switch your way thru building and check logical locations and operation of switches.

Power Item

Exhaust fans and motors.

Disposal.

Range and ovens.

Refrigerator and freezer.

Washer and dryer.

Hot water heater.

Trash masher.

Hair dryers.

Electric Heat

Locate all heat elements and baseboards to scale.

Thermostats, locate directly above switch. Keep away from sun shining in window.

Heat tape locations.

Key elements to schedule or call them out.

NOTES

Service

Main panel board location close to entrance, must be accessible.

Entrance and meter location must relate to building design.

Draw detail of meter. True and plumb at 54″ above finish grade line.

Miscellaneous Electrical

Door bell and chime location.

Music system—speakers.

T.V. receptacle.

Telephone jacks.

Smoke and heat detector.

Burglar alarm.

Mechanical

Locate furnace or boiler. Check routing of piping and ducting through framing.

Check to see that proper ventilation is specified for gas or propane furnace, boilers and water heaters.

Pan and open drain for hot water heater. Door to water heater 1 hour with 20 ga. G.I. inside.

Pressure reducing valve and pop off valves noted.

Plumbing fixtures shown and keyed to schedule.

Show all exterior freeze proof hose bibs.

Locate water entry and main shut off valves.

Locate all stacks and roof drains.

Dryer vent.

Check sound control on all stacks.

Check to see that all mechanical items miss structure.

Review all heating elements, air diffusers, and return air grilles with furniture and drapery layout.

Floor drains.

Schedules

Light fixture schedule.

Heat element schedule.

Appliance schedule.

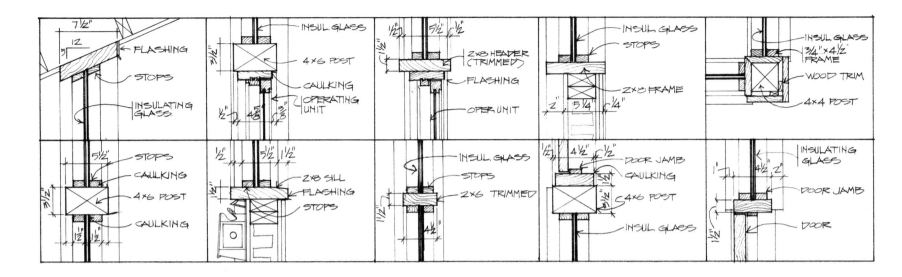

 N **WINDOW DETAILS**
1½"=1'-0"
SEE :

MARK	UNIT DIMENSION	REMARKS
2715	2'-8" × 1'-8"	
2723	2'-8" × 2'-4"	
2731	2'-8" × 3'-0"	
3515	3'-4" × 1'-8"	
3523	3'-4" × 2'-4"	
3531	3'-4" × 3'-0"	
4315	4'-0" × 1'-8"	
OPERATING UNITS NOTED THUS: 		
PROVIDE INSULATING GLASS, ALL UNITS		

O **WINDOW SCHEDULE**

Window details are sectional projections through window panels which described their assembly and connection to the building. While doing this last significant job in the working drawing process, one gains an awareness of how things fit together at the exterior openings of the building, and the final bits of information needed to do the dimensions.

Typically, window frames are built by jobbers in a shop far removed from the building site. People manufacturing the frames have no personal contact with people assembling the building. Window details are the mode of communication between the two parties.

To fulfill this role, window details must be clear and explicit. They are keyed to the building elevations and define all different conditions of assembly, fit, connection, and trim.

WINDOW DETAILS

NOTES

WINDOW DETAILS CHECK LIST

Element Title and Number.
Scale: 1½″ = 1′.
Cross Reference.

Key to exterior elevations.

Layout on same sheet as exterior elevations, keeping space economy in mind.

Show all different conditions—combine jamb and head where practical.

When glass is less than 18″ off floor, safety glass required.

Include detail, showing how frame attaches to rough buck.

Door and window trim.

    Fixed glass stops   1⅜″ × ¾″.

    Door stops   1½″ × ½″.

Standard window trim mill—⅜″ × 2¼″.

Windows in bedrooms must have 22″ × 22″ clear opening per U.B.C.

Show all necessary flashing.

The text and checklist for each element suggested that dimension lines be drawn, but that no dimensions be applied. Numbers have been deferred until this point in the process so that more complete information would be available. Knowledge of all the ramifications of the dimensions has grown as each element was drawn. The draftsman should be fully prepared to handle them at this time.

Dimensions are numbers which represent the measurements that describe the building and the location of its parts. The builder relies on the dimensions to lay out the work, and to fit all the parts of the building together. Dimensions must be done in a professional manner. They must be complete and correct.

It is best to do the dimensions on a set of prints provided specifically for this purpose. Many adjustments will be made before they are finished. It is quicker and more expedient to make these changes on prints than on original drawings.

Start by doing the horizontal dimensions on the floor plans. Then proceed to the foundation plan and the framing plans. Known dimensions, such as opening sizes are put in first. Next, assumed dimensions, such as room sizes are inserted. Unknown dimensions are determined by adding up the knowns and subtracting from the total. When complete, all dimensions between the same two points should amount to the same sum.

NOTES

Upon completion of the horizontal dimensions, move on to the verticals. Fill in all the elevations and dimension lines on the cross sections, wall sections, elevations, and details.

When the dimensions have been completed on the set of prints, they should be completely and thoroughly checked. Upon satisfaction of this requirement, they can be transferred to the original drawings.

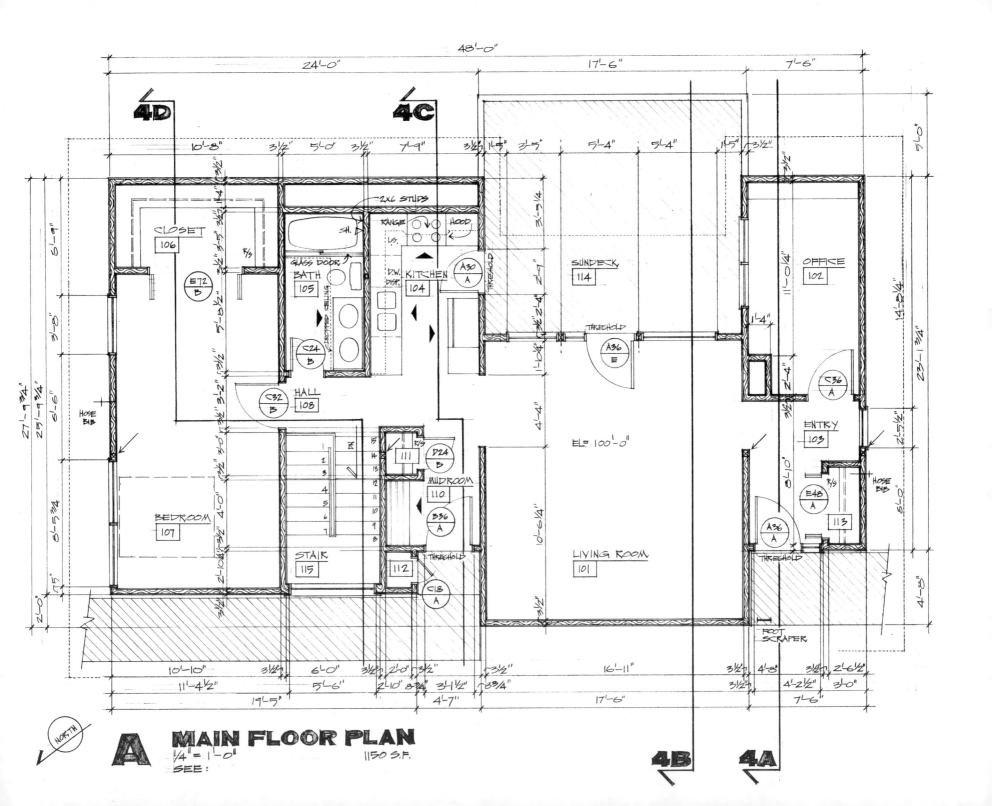

MAIN FLOOR PLAN

A

1/4" = 1'-0"
SEE:

1150 S.F.

NORTH

4D   4C

4B   4A

CLOSET
106

BATH
105

KITCHEN
104

SUNDECK
114

OFFICE
102

HALL
108

ENTRY
103

BEDROOM
107

MUDROOM
110

LIVING ROOM
101

STAIR
115

112

RANGE   HOOD

GLASS DOOR

2x6 STUDS

SH.

D.W. DISP.

DROPPED CEILING

THRESHOLD

THRESHOLD

THRESHOLD

THRESHOLD

FOOT SCRAPER

HOSE BIB

HOSE BIB

R/S

R/S

R/S

EL= 100'-0"

E72 B

C24 B

C32 B

A30 A

A36 E

C36 A

E48 A

A36 A

B36 A

D24 B

C18 A

111

113

NOTES

DIMENSIONS CHECK LIST

Floor Plans

Overall dimensions.

   Dimensions to wall breaks.

   To windows and openings.

      Rough opening +2″ for doors.

      Allow for double stud ea. side of doors.

      Per schedule for windows.

   To structural items.

   To all partitions.

   Dimension wall thickness (actual stud width).

   Balconies, stairs, and miscellaneous.

   Fireplace hearth.

   Show floor el. = at each floor.

Foundation Plan

Overall dimensions.

Footing extensions.

To all breaks in wall.

To all openings.

Caisson or pad footing layout.

Wall thickness and footing widths.

To steps in walls and footings.

Show top of wall, el.= for each change of elevation.

Show top of footing or caisson el.= thus, ( ) for each change in elevation.

Show horizontal dimension on details.

Show wall and footing elevations on details.

Framing Plans

Overall dimensions.

To all bearing lines and columns.

To all openings requiring a beam.

To edge of all framing systems.

Beam lengths.

To center of beams for layout.

Bearing wall thicknesses.

Beam bearing lengths.

Overhang beams and joists.

Top of floor el.= in notes.

Top of beam el.= where not obvious.

NOTES

Cross Sections

Show el.= at each floor line.

Show el.= at each rafter bearing point.

Roof slopes.

Stair dimensions.

    Show number and tread sizes with total dimension.

    Show number and riser sizes with total dimension.

    Show landing dimension.

    Interior railing dimensions.

    Dimension slab and gravel.

    Identify work point for all dimensions and elevations, if not obvious.

Elevations

Show el.= at each floor line.

Show el.= at each rafter bearing point.

Roof slopes.

Dimension all projections from building.

    Roof overhangs.

Balconies.

Beams.

Chimneys.

Dimension porch and balcony railings.

Site Plan

Property line lengths and bearings.

Overall dimensions of building.

Set back dimensions.

Show el.= of main floor.

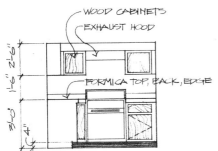

WOOD CABINETS
EXHAUST HOOD
FORMICA TOP, BACK, EDGE

2'-6"
1'-6"
3'-0"
4"

A KITCHEN
SCALE: 1/4" = 1'-0"

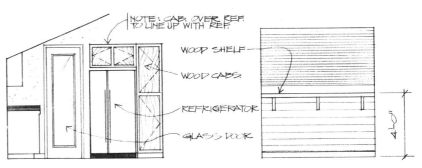

NOTE: CAB. OVER REF. TO LINE UP WITH REF.

WOOD SHELF
WOOD CABS.
REFRIGERATOR
GLASS DOOR

4'-0"

B KITCHEN
SCALE: 1/4" = 1'-0"

C OFFICE
SCALE: 1/4" = 1'-0"

DROPPED CEILING

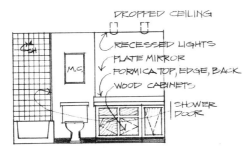

RECESSED LIGHTS
PLATE MIRROR
FORMICA TOP, EDGE, BACK
WOOD CABINETS
SHOWER DOOR

M.C.

D BATH
SCALE: 1/4" = 1'-0"

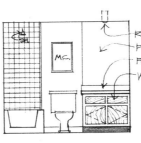

RECESSED LIGHTS
PLATE MIRROR
FORMICA TOP, EDGE, BACK
WOOD CABINET

M.C.

E BATH
SCALE: 1/4" = 1'-0"

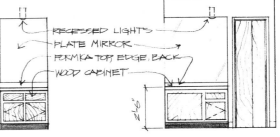

2'-6"

F LAV.
SCALE: 1/4" = 1'-0"

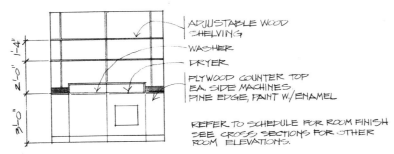

ADJUSTABLE WOOD SHELVING
WASHER
DRYER
PLYWOOD COUNTER TOP EA. SIDE MACHINES, PINE EDGE, PAINT W./ENAMEL

REFER TO SCHEDULE FOR ROOM FINISH
SEE CROSS SECTIONS FOR OTHER ROOM ELEVATIONS.

1'-4"
2'-0"
3'-0"

G LAUNDRY
SCALE: 1/4" = 1'-0"

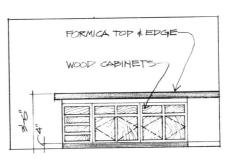

FORMICA TOP & EDGE
WOOD CABINETS

3'-6"
4"

H BAR
SCALE: 1/4" = 1'-0"

Interior elevations are vertical projections of walls inside the building which have cabinets, millwork, or special features attached. These are shown as part of the sections wherever possible.

This step comes towards the end of the process because the items described do not affect the structure or construction of the building. This work is attached or applied to the space provided. It is logical to do these drawings after the building is fully developed on paper.

The builder uses the interior elevations to estimate the cabinet work, and to guide him in its installation. The information which he needs to know is summarized on the check lists which follow.

NOTES

INTERIOR ELEVATIONS CHECK LIST

Element Title and Number.
Scale: ¼″ = 1′.
Cross Reference.

Locate on same sheet as floor plan and room finish schedule if possible. Utilize cross sections to show room elevations where feasible.

Verify with room finish schedule and door schedule and floor plans.

Show all cabinets, shelves, and millwork.

Show all appliances and fixtures.

Range and oven with hood.

Sinks—dashed line.

Refrigerator.

Dishwasher.

Trash masher.

Disposal—dashed line.

Washer and dryer.

Call Out

Formica tops, ceramic tile backs.

Wood or formica edges.

See schedule for wall finish.

Wood cabinets.

Base, rubber or wood.

Dropped ceilings.

Under cabinet lighting.

Dimensions

Vertical dimensions of cabinets and custom millwork.

Mounting heights of fixtures.

Miscellaneous Items

Be sure there is clarification on whether or not contractor supplies appliances.

Note cabinet manufacturer and cabinet quality by reference to specifications.

Check to see that inside corners have 3"–4" minimum clearance so drawers do not conflict.

Check to see that lazy susan has minimum of 1' at inside corner.

Show cabinet hinges, dashed line.

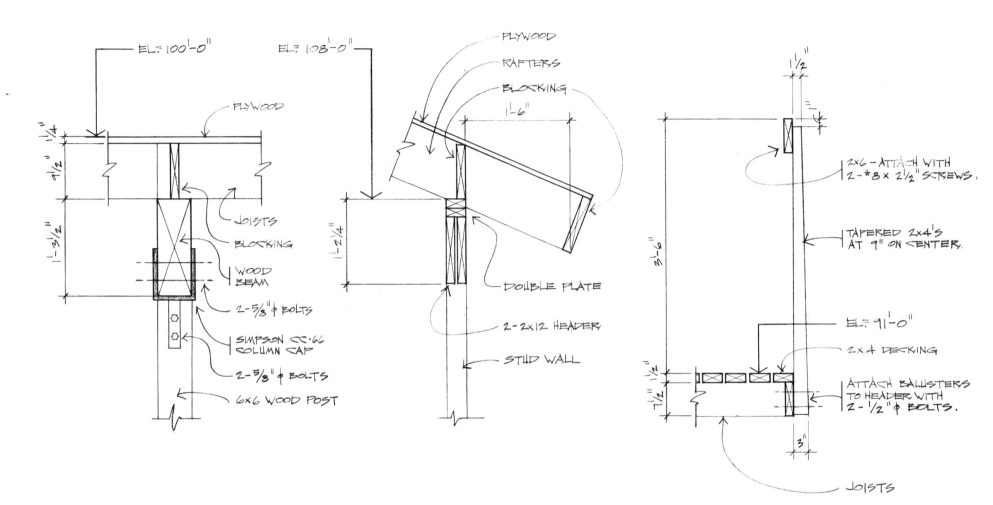

EL.= 100'-0"

EL.= 108'-0"

1/4"

7 1/2"

1'-3 1/2"

PLYWOOD

JOISTS

BLOCKING

WOOD BEAM

2-5/8"⌀ BOLTS

SIMPSON CC·66 COLUMN CAP

2-5/8"⌀ BOLTS

6x6 WOOD POST

PLYWOOD

RAFTERS

BLOCKING

1'-6"

1'-2 1/4"

DOUBLE PLATE

2-2x12 HEADER

STUD WALL

1 1/2"

3'-6"

1 1/2"

7 1/2"

3"

2x6 - ATTACH WITH 2-#8 x 2 1/2" SCREWS.

TAPERED 2x4's AT 9" ON CENTER.

EL.= 91'-0"

2x4 DECKING

ATTACH BALUSTERS TO HEADER WITH 2-1/2"⌀ BOLTS.

JOISTS

 P  **DETAIL**
3/4"=1'-0"
SEE:

 Q **DETAIL**
3/4"=1'-0"
SEE:

 R **DETAIL**
3/4"=1'-0"
SEE

A complete picture of the building has now been drawn. Some points will still require emphasis however. This is done with details.

Details are projections of various types which show enlargements of selected portions of the building. They are drawn to clarify places where particular attention is needed in the process of construction.

The check list gives some idea of the details which may be required. Common sense and experience will call for others. Details should be clearly drawn to show the information intended. Building parts which are irrelevant and detract from the purpose of the detail should be omitted.

DETAILS

MISCELLANEOUS DETAILS CHECK LIST

Element Title and Number.
Scale: ½″ = 1′-0″ concrete
       ¾″ = 1′-0″ wood and steel.
       ⅜″ = 1′-0″ stairs.
Cross Reference.

Cut details only where necessary to clarify connections and items called out elsewhere. Many details can be blown up from cross sections.

Dimensions

Show elevation at one dimensioned point.

Dimension off of this point show only those dimensions which pertain to the purpose of this detail.

Show Only Those Materials Which Pertain to the Purpose of the Detail

Show Weld Symbols

Details Usually Necessary

Framing connections.

Balcony railing.

Stairs.

   Railing.

   Tread.

   Rise and run dimensions.

Stair frame.

Connections.

Kick blocking.

Flashing.

To chimney and fireplace.

Metal beam caps.

Valley flashing.

Gravel Stop Detail

Paper folded over edge.

Metal applied over paper.

Tar and gravel on top.

Cold Roof

Ridge vent.

Show all parts.

Felt over sheathing and below shakes.

Thickened Slab

Steel Beams

Connections.

Stiffeners.

Bearing plates (minimum bearing 6″–8″).

Embeco grout at bearing.

Weld symbols.

Steel Columns

Cap and base plates.

Weld symbols.

Dimensions so that fabricator determines length.

Specifications describe the quality of materials, the types of products, and the nature of craftsmanship required in the construction of a building. The drawings are graphic. They show how much, where, what size, and how to put it together. Drawings relate to quantity. Specifications relate to quality. Together with the drawings, they describe the building.

Now the true nature and fabric of the building is known. Decisions on quality have been made and recorded while its image was growing. With this picture in mind, the specifications may be easily and efficiently written.

Both the drawings and the specifications have their respective functions, which should not overlap. Each tells its own story. Specifications should be written in a clear direct manner, using simple language familiar to the tradesmen doing the work. They should be comprehensive, and completely describe all the ramifications of the project.

The accompanying guide breaks the specifications down into sixteen sections, each covering a separate aspect of the building project. The guide is designed to help the writer include all the information needed to describe the work. Items normally specified are listed, unique items must be added in the appropriate section.

SPECIFICATIONS

NOTES

When the nature of an item is not determined at the time specifications are written, an allowance may be used in lieu of its description. An allowance is a budgeted amount of money added to the estimate to cover the cost of a particular item. When the material is supplied, the allowance is adjusted to reflect the difference between the cost of the item and the budgeted amount.

SPECIFICATIONS

1. General Requirements

a. This contract shall be written on AIA Form #____, with AIA General Conditions, AIA 201, in effect as if written out in full. The scope of the work shall include _____.

b. All work shall comply with state and local codes and ordinances, and shall be done to the highest standards of craftsmanship by journeymen of the respective trades.

c. Samples shall be supplied to the architect of all materials proposed for substitution of specified materials, and of workmanship representing artistic techniques specified below. Shop drawings shall be provided for fabricated items specified below.

d. Temporary facilities for protection of tools and equipment shall conform to local regulations, and shall be the contractor's responsibility.

e. Contractor shall present the building to the owner for acceptance, clean and ready for occupancy. All glass shall be cleaned and polished, floors swept broom clean, carpets vacuumed, fixtures washed, with all labels removed, and exterior hand raked free of trash and debris.

NOTES

f. Winter protection, heat, and snow removal shall be the contractor's responsibility. All space heating shall be done in a safe, sensible manner, with periodic checks on the systems, and shall comply with state industrial commission and O.S.H.A. regulations.

g. Contractor shall erect a 2' × 4' sign lettered by a professional sign painter, identifying the project, the architect, the contractors, and the lending agency.

h. Contractor shall submit a schedule of values, as outlined in Article 9.2.1 of the General Conditions, on the form provided by the architect at the time of signing this contract.

i. Bond requirements.

j. Contractor shall carry builders risk "All Risk" insurance to cover the cost of this work and all coverage as defined in Article 11 of the General Conditions. Architect shall be presented with certificates of contractor's insurance and owner's fire and extended coverage at the time of signing of the contract.

k. Rental charges, safety, protection, and maintenance of rented equipment shall be the contractor's responsibility.

l. Contractor shall maintain the job clear of trash and debris as defined in Article 4.16 of the General Conditions. All waste materials shall be removed from site prior to substantial completion and prior to final acceptance.

m. Costs for building permits, landfill taxes, use tax, sales tax, and other charges relative to construction of this project shall be included in the contract price.

n. These documents do not include the necessary components for construction safety. Safety, care of adjacent properties during construction, compliance with state and federal regulations regarding safety, and compliance with Article 10 of the General Conditions is, and shall be, the contractor's responsibility.

o. Contractor shall visit the site and become familiar with all conditions prior to submitting his proposal. Contractor shall verify all dimensions and conditions shown on these drawings with those at the site. Any variation which requires physical change shall be brought to the attention of the architect.

2. Site Work
Contractor shall provide necessary labor, materials, and equipment to perform all site work shown on specified in these documents.

a. Strip site of existing topsoil and stockpile for reuse in landscaping. All trees designated on site plan shall be protected from damage of construction processes and machines.

b. Regrade drive and parking area and provide 16" compacted bed of approved pit run gravel.

c. Excavate, fill, and regrade site to finish grades noted on site plan. Spread uniform layer of existing topsoil over entire re-graded area. Provide fences, barricades, and/or lights around all open trenches, excavations, and other hazards.

d. Backfilling operations are the responsibility of the contractor. Foundation walls shall be adequately braced before backfilling. All backfill materials shall be approved granular materials compacted to 90% proctor density.

e. Provide road drainage and storm culverts as shown on the site plan.

f. All utility lines shall be extended from building to utility connection. Connection charges shall be included in cost of this work.

g. Provide 4″ perimeter foundation drain and underdrain in compliance with soils engineer recommendations.

h. Provide all exterior walks, steps, and patios as shown on the site plan.

i. All drive and parking bed gravel to be pit run. Drain tile and surface gravel to be washed and graded ¾″ to 1½″.

j. Concrete walks, curbs, retaining walls, and other site amenities shall comply with section 3 of this specification.

k. All disturbed vegetation and ground cover shall be reseeded with native grasses and mulched with a layer of straw. Transplant seedlings, shrubs, and trees noted on the site plan.

3. Concrete

Contractor shall provide all necessary labor, materials, and equipment to complete all concrete shown or noted in these documents.

a. All concrete for slabs, footings, and caissons shall develop 3,000 PSI in 28 days. All concrete for prefabricated structure shall be as required by codes and loading conditions specified with shop drawings.

b. All concrete form work shall be adequately tied together and braced to form true lines, square corners, and plumb walls.

c. All footings shall be formed to meet sizes indicated on drawings, details, and/or schedules.

d. Caissons shall be drilled in conformance with the foundation plan, schedules, and details. Caisson holes subject to seeping or silting shall be pumped and cleaned prior to pouring concrete. Concrete shall be poured and vibrated so as to eliminate air pockets.

e. All reinforcing bars shall conform to A.S.T.M. spec (A 625) deformed bars with a minimum yield stress of 40,000 PSI (60,000 PSI). Welded wire fabric shall be 6 × 6, 10/10, conforming to A.S.T.M. Spec 185.

f. Cast in place concrete shall be poured continuously, with no cold joints. Material shall be adequately vibrated to prevent the occurrence of air pockets and honeycomb effects.

g. Poured footings shall be poured on undisturbed soil, as described in the soil report as bearing material, regardless of elevations shown or noted on drawings.

h. Concrete walls shall be pointed at all ties and blemishes with sand and cement grout. Exposed surface finish to be _____.

i. Concrete slabs shall be poured on compacted materials, described in the soils report. Slab surfaces shall be smooth and level, or shall have smooth even slope to floor drains. Concrete finish shall be _____ for interior floor slabs, _____ for exterior walks and stairs.

j. Concrete stairs shall have 1° sloped risers with metal edge nosing and _____ finish.

k. No concrete shall be poured subject to freezing conditions or on frozen ground.

l. Structural concrete.

m. Pre-stressed and pre-cast concrete.

4. Masonry

Contractor shall provide necessary labor, materials, and equipment to lay up masonry as shown or specified in these documents. All work shall be laid plumb, true and square with filled joints.

a. Stucco shall be freshly prepared and uniformly mixed in the ratio by volume of 1 part cement, 1 part lime putty, and 6 parts sand. All stucco shall be applied to clean, moist concrete and masonry surfaces.

b. Mortar shall be freshly prepared and uniformly mixed in the ratio by volumes of 1 part cement, ½ part lime putty, 4½ parts sand, and shall conform to A.S.T.M. Spec 270. If plastic type cement is used, the lime putty shall be omitted.

c. Grout shall be of fluid consistency and mixed in the ratio by volumes, one part cement, three parts sand, and 2 parts pea gravel.

d. Sample masonry section of minimum 16 sq. ft. shall be laid up for approval of architect. Sample section may be a portion of the contracted work.

e. Masonry units shall be sound, dry, clean, and free from cracks. Concrete block shall be grade A units conforming to A.S.T.M. designation C-90.
Brick shall be as manufactured by _____.
Stone shall be _____ as quarried by _____.

f. Horizontal reinforcing shall be standard dur.o.wal. Vertical reinforcing shall be A.S.T.M. Spec A-615. Deformed bars with minimum yield stress of 40,000 psi.

g. Joint treatment to be _____.

h. All walls shall be adequately braced until securely tied to the structure. No work shall be done subject to freezing conditions.

NOTES

5. Metals

Contractor shall provide necessary labor materials and equipment to erect all miscellaneous iron and steel as detailed or noted on these drawings.

a. Shop drawings are required for all structural steel, railings, and _____. All structural steel shall be detailed and fabricated in accordance with the latest edition of the A.I.S.C. Manual of Steel Construction. Use standard framed beam connections unless otherwise noted.

b. Structural steel shall conform to A.S.T.M. Spec A 36, except pipe columns, which shall conform to A.S.T.M. Spec A 53.

c. Metal decking shall be _____.

d. Hand railings, mud scrapers, and other miscellaneous iron to be supplied by _____.

e. Metal J mold trim, beam caps, foundation caps to be 22 GA galvanized metal by local craftsmen.

f. Steel stair to be model # _____ by _____.

g. Built in metal fireplace to be _____ by _____.

108

6. Carpentry

Contractor shall provide all labor, materials, and equipment to frame up, sheath, and trim out building as shown or specified in these documents.

Framing: framing lumber shall be stress graded, kiln dried Douglas Fir or Larch.

a. Joists and rafters shall be a stress graded "No.1."; Truss Joists to be as manufactured by Truss Joist Corporation. Manufacturer shall supply all accessories.

b. Wood beams shall be stress graded No. 1. Glulam beams shall be _____.

c. Stud walls shall be 2 × _____'s stress graded studs.

d. Wood blocking shall be solid and match the depth of main members. Framing plans show members required for structural purposes only, all blocking and members required by codes are in addition to members shown.

e. Wood stairs shall be stress graded No. 1.

f. Floor sheathing shall be exterior grade CD T & G plywood or ¾" red × redwood particle board. Wood decking shall be _____ select spruce (fir).

g. Roof sheathing shall be exterior grade C/D plywood. Wood decking shall be _____ select spruce (fir).

h. Exterior wall sheathing shall be ½" asphalt impregnated fibre board, except at corners, which shall be one full sheet exterior grade C/D plywood. Cover with 6 mil poly vinyl film moisture barrier.

i. Cold roof to be 1 × 3 pine furring, @ 16" vertical 8" horizontal.

j. All framing connections to be by Simpson Company or local shop meeting same configuration.

Finish—All finish work to be executed by trained journeymen and shall be filled, sanded smooth, and ready for painter.

a. Wood fascia to be _____.
Back painted and screwed at corners.

b. Soffits and exterior ceilings to be _____.

c. Exterior siding to be _____.

d. Exterior trim to be _____.

e. Balcony railings to be _____.

f. Exterior decking to be _____.

g. Interior wood paneling to be _____.

h. Interior wood trim to be _____.

i. Interior railing to be _____.

j. Stair treads to be _____.

k. Wood flooring to be _____.

l. Closet shelving to be _____.

m. Mill work shall be _____.

n. Wood cabinets shall be _____.

7. Thermal & Moisture Protection

Contractor shall provide all labor, materials, and equipment to install insulation, roof, and waterproofing as detailed or specified in these documents.

a. Batt insulation to be _____ in walls, _____ in roof, _____ in floors, and _____ in bathroom walls.

b. Rigid insulation to be _____ inside walls below slab, _____ inside concrete or masonry walls, _____ on roof.

c. Foam insulation to be _____.

d. Built up roof to be JM spec _____ with _____ gravel.

e. Metal roof to be _____ GA _____, colored _____ attached with _____.

f. Cedar shakes/shingles to be _____ installed strictly in accordance with manufacturers instructions.

g. Waterproof deck to be _____.

h. Special roofing to be _____.

i. All flashing to be 24 Ga. G.I. metal. Gravel stops and beam caps to be 22 Ga. G.I. metal.

j. Roof accessories to be _____.

k. Foundation to be dampproofed/water proofed with _____, provide glass fab at all inside corners.

l. All caulking to be _____, colored _____.

8. Doors, Windows, and Glass

Contractor shall supply and install all doors, windows, and glazing as detailed, scheduled, and/or specified in these documents.

Doors—All doors to be equipped with hardware as defined in the hardware schedule, shall be sealed, top, bottom, and all sides, as defined in Section 9, and shall be operating snug and smoothly.

a. Exterior doors to be _____ with _____ frames and _____ trim. All exterior doors to be caulked and weatherstripped with hidden aluminum spring strip and shall have _____ weatherproof threshold.

b. Interior doors to be _____ with _____ frames and _____ trim.

c. Glass sliding doors to be _____ by _____ with _____ glass.

d. Folding doors to be _____ by _____ with _____.

e. Overhead doors to be _____ by _____ with _____.

f. Storm and screen doors to be _____ by _____ with _____ screen/glass. Storm doors to be weatherstripped.

Windows—All windows to be caulked and weatherstripped, sealed on all edges and surfaces as defined in Section 9, and shall be operating snug and smoothly.

a. Operating windows to be _____ by _____ with _____ glass and _____ trim.

b. Wood window frames to be _____ by _____ with _____ and _____ trim.

c. Exterior glazing to be _____ in all fixed frames and operating units.

d. Interior glazing to be _____ glass. Safety glass and tempered glass where required by code.

e. Mirrors to be _____.

f. Glass shower doors to be _____ by _____.

9. Finishes

Contractor shall provide all material and labor to finish interior rooms and building exterior, as shown, noted, scheduled, or specified in these documents.

a. Plaster to be _____ thick with _____ finish.

b. Drywall to be ½″ thick, taped, filled, and sanded smooth. Firecode drywall shall be ⅝″ thick on ceilings and ½″ thick on walls, taped, filled, and sanded smooth.

c. Drywall texture to be _____ on walls and _____ on ceilings.

d. Wood paneling to be _____.

e. Ceramic tile _____.

f. Wall covering to be _____.

g. Ceiling tiles to be _____.

h. Carpet to be _____ with _____ pad _____.

i. Wood flooring to be _____.

j. Quarry tile to be _____.

k. Sheet flooring to be _____.

l. Asphalt or rubber tile _____.

m. Rubber base to be _____.

n. Rubber stair treads to be _____.

o. Plastic laminate tops to be by _____. Refer to schedule for color and location.

p. All painting and varnish shall be a 2 coat job of the highest quality workmanship, free of runs and sags, with straight cuts. Where painting occurs over existing work, one opaque white coat shall precede two coats of color. All stain shall be 1 coat.

1. Exterior siding, soffit, beams, and railings _____.

2. Wood fascia _____.

3. Exterior windows and doors and miscellaneous trim
_____.

4. Cedar shakes _____.

5. Metal roofing and flashing _____.

6. Metal gravel stops, beam caps, and other miscellaneous metal _____.

7. Interior walls and ceilings _____.

8. Interior wood trim and shelving _____.

9. Interior doors _____ sealed top, bottom, and all sides.

10. Wood flooring _____.

11. Wood hand railings _____.

12. Wood cabinets and millwork _____.

10. Specialty Items

Contractor shall provide all labor and materials to install the specialty items, shown, noted, or specified in these documents.

a. Free standing unit fireplace shall be model _____ by _____.

b. Bath accessories and kitchen accessories shall be by _____

_____, _____. Refer to hardware schedule for items required.

c. Hardware to be by _____. Refer to hardware schedule for items required.

d. Moveable partitions to be by _____, colored _____.

e. Disappearing stairs _____.

f. Clothes rods and curtain rods _____.

11. Equipment

Contractor shall provide all labor and materials to install equipment shown, noted, or specified in these documents.

a. Residential appliances, refer to schedule for specific items. All appliances by _____.

b. Pre-finished wood cabinets, refer to schedule for specific items. Wood cabinets to be _____ by _____ finish. Provide all backing and filler items pre-finished to match cabinets.

12. Furnishings

Contractor shall provide all labor and materials to install the following items.

13. Special Construction

Contractor shall provide all labor and materials to install the following items:

a. Pre-fab buildings

b. Swimming pools

c. Incinerators

d. Sky domes

14. Conveying Systems

Contractor shall provide all labor and materials to install the following items:

a. Elevators

b. Dumbwaiters

c. Escalators

15. Mechanical

Contractor shall provide all labor, materials, and equipment necessary to install plumbing, related fixtures, ventilation, roof and floor drains, heating and air conditioning. All work shall comply with state and local codes and ordinances. Subcontractors shall coordinate work with all other trades. Terminal hookup of all fixtures and tap in to all utilities is required. Contractor shall install and check all pressure reducing valves, pop off valves, and other safety devices prior to operation of system.

Plumbing

a. Install domestic hot and cold water supply in copper.

b. Install soil waste and vent system in _____, copper, cast iron, P.V.C.;Building drain from 10' outside house to sewer tap may be vitreous clay pipe.

c. Install roof and floor drains to daylight

117

d. All plumbing fixtures to be by _____, installed in unmarred condition, and protected to completion of work.

e. Hot water heater to be _____ gallon, quick recovery glass lined, fiberglass insulation _____ model by _____.

Heating and Ventilation

a. Heat distribution system to be _____. Convectors, registers by _____, pumps _____ fans.

b. Boiler to be _____ BTU _____ gallon by _____, with metal bestos flue. Furnace to be _____ BTU _____ CFM.

c. Air conditioning _____.

d. Provide _____ combustion air vent and duct to boiler furnace and gas hot water heaters.

e. Exhaust fans to be _____ CFM _____ by _____. Refer to heat plan for location.

f. Install _____ thermostat and control.

16. Electrical
Contractor shall provide and install all labor, materials, and equipment necessary to install wiring, related fixtures, electric heat elements, and control. All work shall comply with state and local codes and ordinances. Subcontractor shall coordinate work with all other trades. Terminal hookup is required of all fixtures and appliances, motors, fans, and controls.

Domestic

a. Main panel board to be 200 amp, 40 circuit non-metallic by _____.

b. All wiring to be Romex copper.

c. Refer to schedule for light fixtures. All fixtures and lamps to be complete.

d. Provide wiring and recepticals for 4 speaker quad music.

e. Provide wiring and recepticals for television.

f. Provide burglar alarm system, complete system to be _____ _____ by _____.

g. Exterior lighting to be _____.

Heating

a. All wiring to be Romex copper.

b. Provide and install all electric heat elements strictly in accordance with manufacturers instructions. Heat elements to be _____.

c. Heat tape shall be U.L. approved.

PART THREE

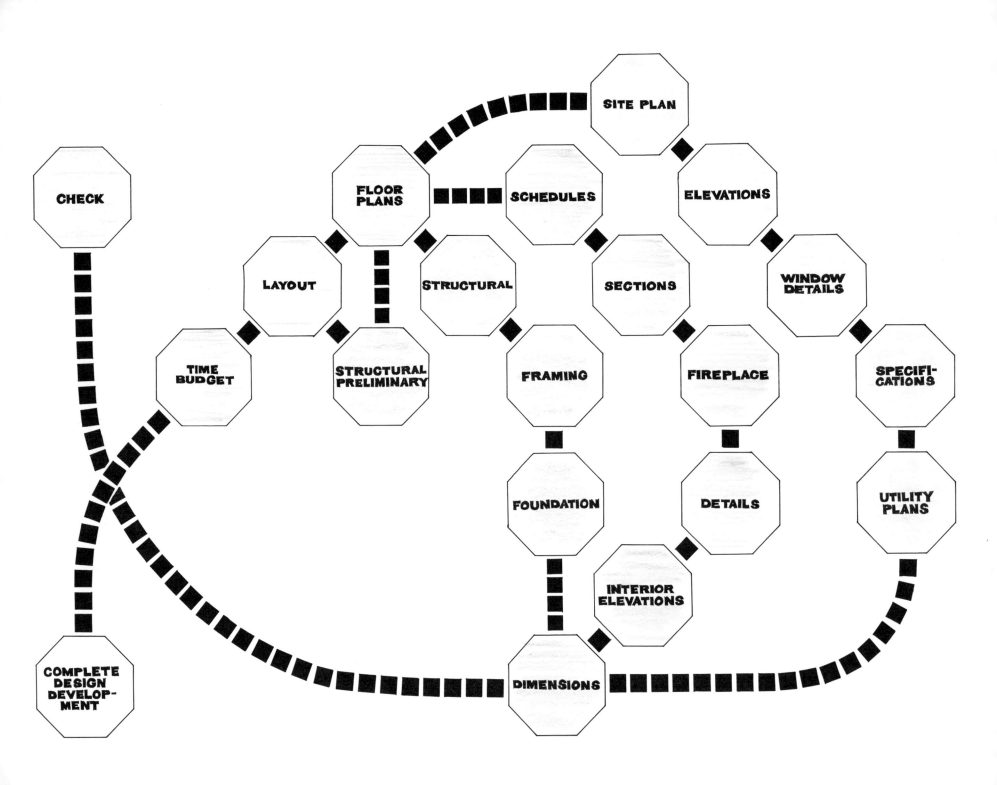

The process described in Part Two depicts one person doing a set of working drawings. This is an idealized situation. However, in most cases, it is not practical for one person to do all of the work. Team drafting is the utilization of a number of people to accomplish the same objectives in less time.

On the preceding page is a flow chart which shows how the process may be revised to include more than one person in the drafting process. Three people are represented, one of whom is the leader.

Budgeting, layout, and floor plans are done by the leader. When he has sufficient information and has established all conditions, others are utilized in the process. As a three person team, they work simultaneously to bring the drawings up to the dimension phase. The lead person then resumes control and sees the job through to completion.

Verbal cross referencing is an important element of team drafting. Team members must communicate with each other in order to check the consistency and progress of the work. The flow chart helps them to see where their contributions fit into the total scope of the job.

Each project is unique. The job itself will have its own conditions, and the number of people available to do the work will vary. A flow chart should be developed for each drawing project, reflecting the conditions and the number of persons available to do the work.

TEAM DRAFTING

The process is best learned by one person doing all of the steps, the idealized situation. In doing so, he or she will be able to see how the drawing of one element will interface with the element which follows. As training, an inexperienced draftsman might take a small project through its complete cycle. Once the process is mastered, the trainee is ready to participate in team drafting.

Reproduction drafting is the employment of copying techniques to make reproducible prints of repetitive drawn elements. This concept is used to save layout time and drafting time.

Floor plans, being the most basic element, are drawn three or more times in the process. Each re-drawing is done to emphasize a particular kind of information. Plans are drawn as the key element for reference, dimensioning, and scheduling. They are used again to show the framing layout and again to describe the electrical elements.

Re-drawing the plan can be eliminated by utilization of reproduction techniques. An example sequence is as follows:

a. First, draw the basic plan, showing only the bearing walls and appropriate dimension lines.

b. Make a reproducible print, such as a sepia. This copy may be used as the basis for a framing plan.

c. Develop the basic plan further, drawing in all partitions, doors, and room identification.

d. Make a second reproducible print, which will be transformed into the utility plan.

e. Finish the basic plan according to the Floor Plan check list.

Reproduction drafting techniques are easy to learn. The key to utilization is the proper equipment and reproduction papers. These things are normally available in an Architect's office. Using them to advantage is a simple step. Once the basics are learned, many opportunities to utilize the same techniques will manifest themselves.

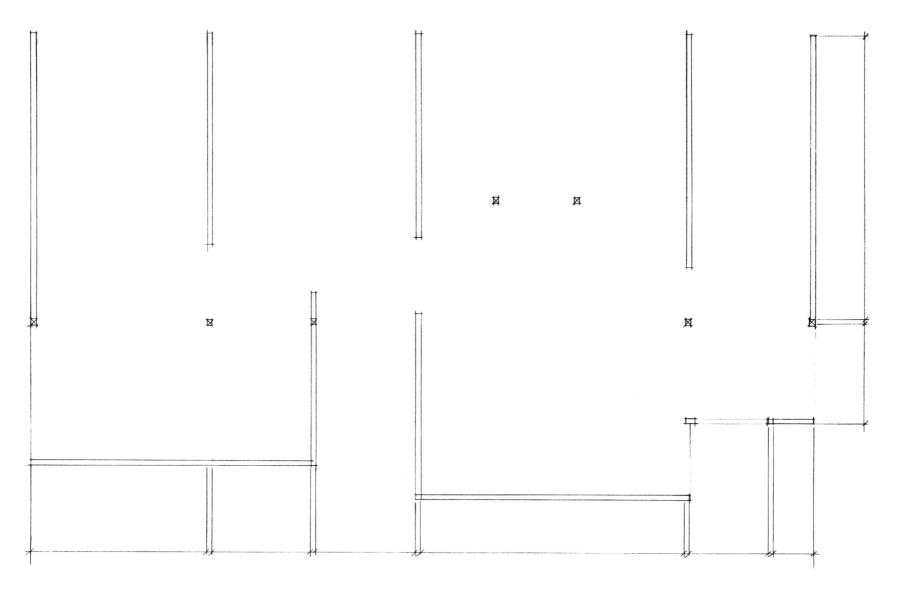

NORTH

**STEP A: DRAW BEARING WALLS AND MAKE
A REPRODUCIBLE PRINT.**

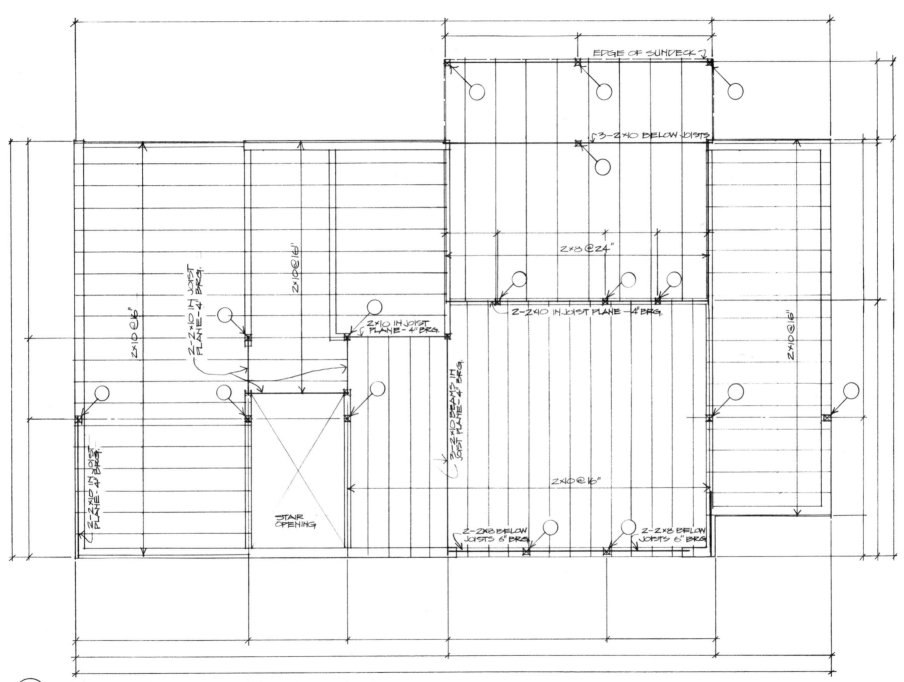

EDGE OF SUNDECK

3-2×10 BELOW JOISTS

2×8 @ 24"

2-2×10 IN JOIST PLANE - 4" BRG.

2×10 @ 16"

2-2×10 IN JOIST PLANE - 4" BRG.

2×10 IN JOIST PLANE - 4" BRG.

2×10 @ 16"

2×10 @ 16"

3-2×10 BEAM IN JOIST PLANE - 4" BRG.

2-2×10 IN JOIST PLANE - 4" BRG.

2×10 @ 16"

STAIR OPENING

2-2×8 BELOW JOISTS 6" BRG.

2-2×8 BELOW JOISTS 6" BRG.

NORTH

H FLOOR FRAMING PLAN
1/4" = 1'-0"
SEE:

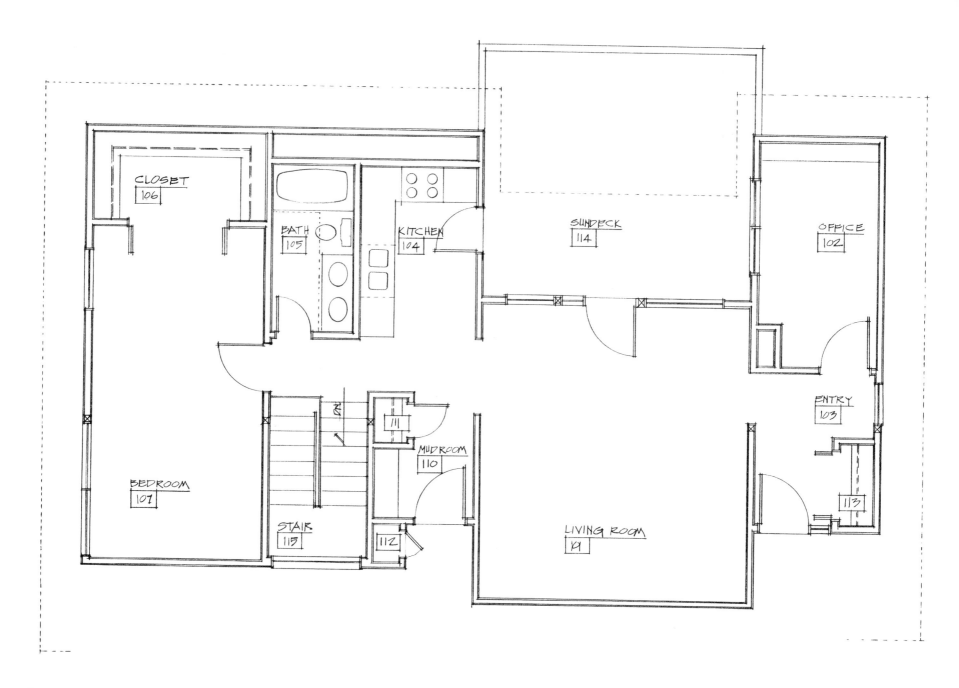

CLOSET
106

BATH
105

KITCHEN
104

SUNDECK
114

OFFICE
102

BEDROOM
107

DN

111

MUDROOM
110

ENTRY
103

STAIR
115

112

113

LIVING ROOM
101

NORTH

STEP C: DEVELOP THE PLAN FURTHER AND MAKE
A SECOND REPRODUCIBLE PRINT.

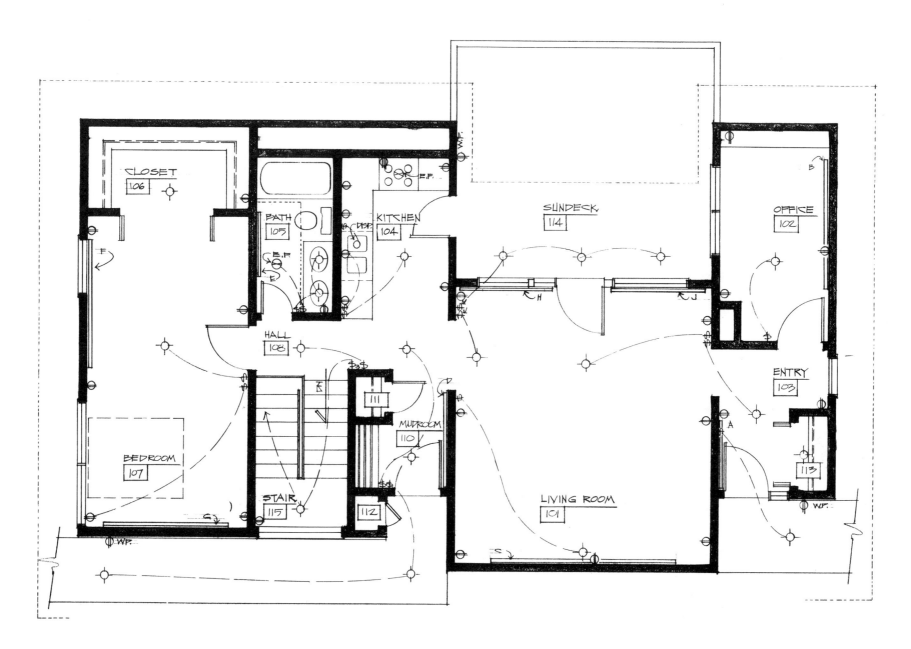

CLOSET
106

BATH
105

KITCHEN
104

SUNDECK
114

OFFICE
102

HALL
108

ENTRY
103

111

MUDROOM
110

BEDROOM
107

STAIR
115

112

LIVING ROOM
101

113

 M **UTILITY PLAN**
1/4"=1'-0"
SEE:

**STEP D: DRAW UTILITY PLAN ON
REPRODUCIBLE PRINT.**

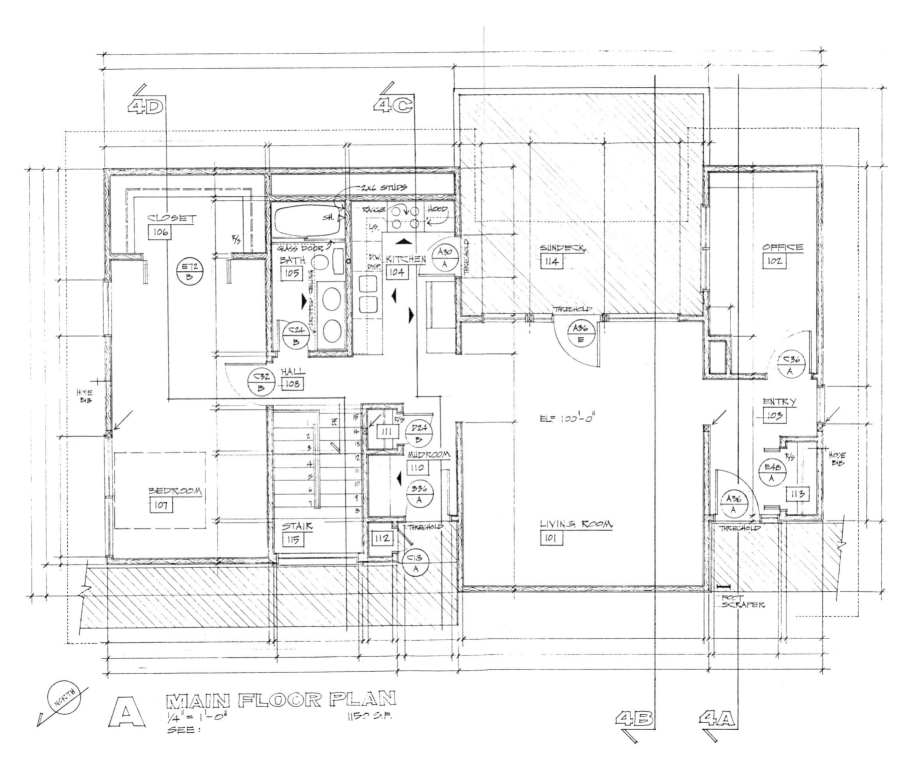

STEP E: FINISH BASIC PLAN ACCORDING TO CHECK LIST.

Planning and control of production time in a design office are important considerations. The influx of jobs is never constant, many jobs will overlap, some being in the schematic phase, others in production, while some may be under construction. Despite these irregularities, the Architect is expected to meet schedules over which he has little control. In addition, he is compelled to keep his staff supplied with a steady flow of work.

The working drawings phase is perhaps the most critical in regard to planning. Project commitments have usually been made, bidding dates selected, construction schedules solidified, and deadlines set.

With many parties depending upon the performance of the Architect, he should be able to make realistic commitments, and to meet them once they have been made.

Project planning and control can be accomplished by the Architect with accurate data pertaining to his own office. First, the data must be collected and organized into usable form. Then it may be utilized for planning and control.

Data is extracted from the time cards used by employees involved in the projects. Each person should keep a time card for each job. When the projects are completed, the data is transferred from all the time cards to a job cost summary. When complete, the summary shows how much time was spent on each element of the drawings. Summary information may then be averaged with other project data and tabulated for project planning use. Sample time cards follow the text showing data for three persons working on a small project. The time card information is combined on the job cost summary, which is then used to develop job cost averages.

To plan a project, simply construct a flow chart similar to the one shown for team drafting. Estimated times for each element may be extracted from the job cost averages and superimposed on the flow chart. By adding the number of hours along the separate paths through the flow chart, and observing the maximum, the time for the project may be determined.

Control for the project is set up by transferring the planning data from the flow chart to a calendar. If time cards are kept up to date and compared to the calendar, one knows if he is keeping to the schedule, and any adjustments can be made accordingly. The illustrations which follow show how this is done. Keep in mind that the process has been oversimplified by the assumption that all projects are the same. Data gathered and used in the fashion described should always be qualified.

One way to get a subjective feel for cost data is to write a job analysis report for each project. These reports will bring objective data into focus with the peculiar ramifications of each project, and give the Architect a better basis for planning with the data.

SAMPLE TIME CARD

NOTES

MAY	LAYOUT	FLOOR PLANS	SCHEDULES	SITE PLAN	STRUCTURAL	FOUNDATION	FRAMING	SECTIONS	FIREPLACE	ELEVATIONS	UTILITY PLANS	WINDOW DETAILS	DIMENSIONS	INTERIOR ELEV.	DETAILS	SPECIFICATIONS	CHECK	TOTAL
1																		
2																		
3	6	2																8
4		8																8
5		8																8
6		2	5															7
7								8										8
8																		
9																		
10								8										8
11								4	4									8
12															8			8
13																		
14													6					6
15																		
16																		
17																	8	8
18																	8	8
19																		
20																		
21																		
22																		
23																		
24																		
25																		
26																		
27																		
28																		
29																		
30																		
T	6	20	5	—	—	—	—	20	4	—	—	—	6	—	8	—	16	85

SAMPLE TIME CARD

MAY	LAYOUT	FLOOR PLANS	SCHEDULES	SITE PLAN	STRUCTURAL	FOUNDATION	FRAMING	SECTIONS	FIREPLACE	ELEVATIONS	UTILITY PLANS	WINDOW DETAILS	DIMENSIONS	INTERIOR ELEV.	DETAILS	SPECIFICATIONS	CHECK	TOTAL
1																		
2																		
3																		
4				8														8
5				2						6								8
6										8								8
7										2	6							8
8																		
9																		
10												6		2				8
12																		
12																8		8
13														2				2
14																		
15																		
16																		
17																		
18																		
19																		
20																		
21																		
22																		
23																		
24																		
25																		
26																		
27																		
28																		
29																		
30																		
T	—	—	—	10	—	—	—	—	—	16	6	6	—	4	—	8	—	50

JOB: A
EMPLOYEE: #3
DATE: May 31, 1976   **SAMPLE TIME CARD**   NOTES

MAY	LAYOUT	FLOOR PLANS	SCHEDULES	SITE PLAN	STRUCTURAL	FOUNDATION	FRAMING	SECTIONS	FIREPLACE	ELEVATIONS	UTILITY PLANS	WINDOW DETAILS	DIMENSIONS	INTERIOR ELEV.	DETAILS	SPECIFICATIONS	CHECK	TOTAL
1																		
2																		
3																		
4																		
5																		
6																		
7					8													8
8																		
9																		
10					8													8
11					4	4												8
12						2	6											8
13							2											2
14																		
15																		
16																		
17																		
18																		
19																		
20																		
21																		
22																		
23																		
24																		
25																		
26																		
27																		
28																		
29																		
30																		
T	—	—	—	—	20	6	8	—	—	—	—	—	—	—	—	—	—	34

SAMPLE: JOB COST SUMMARY

JOB: A DATE: May 31, 1976	ESTIMATED HOURS	ACTUAL HOURS	PERCENT
LAYOUT	6	6	4
FLOOR PLANS	18	20	12
SCHEDULES	6	5	3
SITE PLAN	10	10	6
STRUCTURE	24	20	12
FOUNDATION	6	6	4
FRAMING	8	8	5
SECTIONS	18	20	12
FIREPLACE	4	4	1
ELEVATIONS	18	16	9
UTILITY PLANS	6	6	4
WINDOW DETAILS	8	6	4
DIMENSIONS	6	6	4
INTERIOR ELEV.	4	4	1
DETAILS	6	8	5
SPECIFICATIONS	8	8	5
CHECK	14	16	9
TOTAL	170	169	100%

The actual hours for each element are extracted from employee time cards.

SAMPLE: AVERAGE COST FORM

	JOB A	JOB B	JOB C	JOB D	AVERAGE
LAYOUT	6	6	7	5	6
FLOOR PLANS	18	19	10	18	16
SCHEDULES	6	6	6	6	6
SITE PLAN	10	6	9	15	10
STRUCTURE	24	21	28	30	26
FOUNDATION	6	9	5	9	7
FRAMING	8	5	6	8	7
SECTIONS	18	23	19	34	24
FIREPLACE	4	5	4	6	5
ELEVATIONS	18	15	19	20	18
UTILITY PLANS	6	3	4	7	5
WINDOW DETAILS	8	6	9	9	8
DIMENSIONS	6	8	16	11	10
INTERIOR ELEV.	4	5	4	8	5
DETAILS	4	4	8	6	6
SPECIFICATIONS	8	8	7	8	8
CHECK	14	34	26	30	26
TOTAL	170	184	187	230	193

AVERAGE HOURS FOR EACH ELEMENT

Determine the average hours for each element from a group of similar projects. The averages may be used for estimating and planning similar jobs in the future.

see p 123

SUPERIMPOSE ELEMENT AVERAGES ON THE PROJECT FLOW CHART

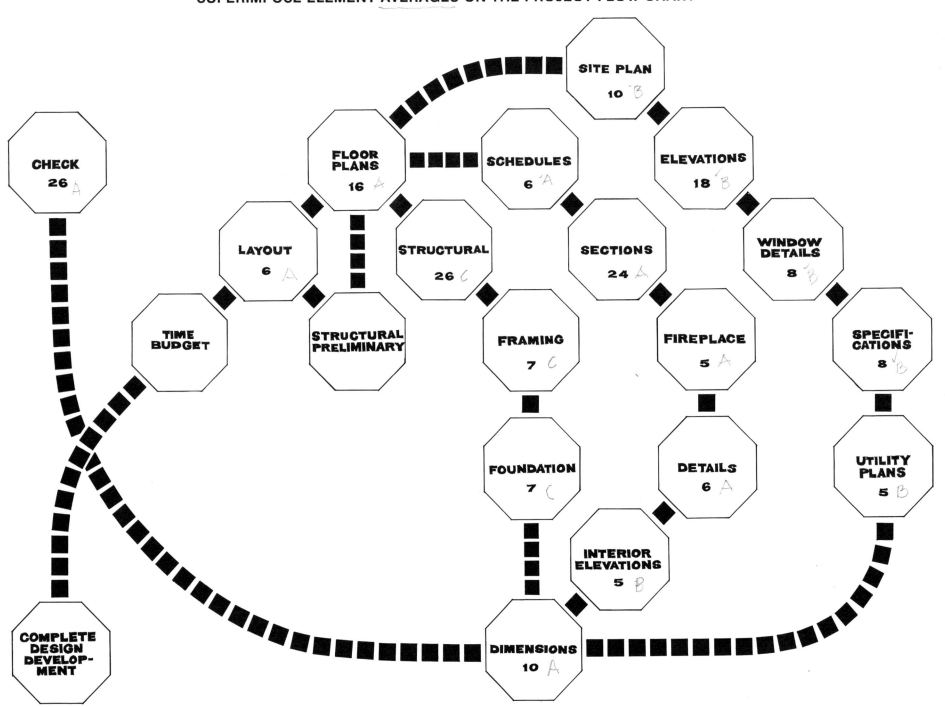

PROJECT CALENDAR

MONDAY	TUESDAY	WEDNESDAY	THURSDAY	FRIDAY
			1	2
3 LAYOUT	4 SITE PLAN	5 FINISH PLANS	6 ELEVATIONS	7
8	9	10	11 SECTIONS	12 SPECI-
13 FICATIONS	14	15	16	17 CHECK
18	19 FINISH JOB	20	21	22
23	24	25	26	27
28	29	30		

Transfer project planning data from the flow chart to a project calendar.

SAMPLE: JOB ANALYSIS REPORT

JOB: A

DATE: MAY 31, 1976

REPORTED BY: JOB CAPTAIN

DESCRIPTION: Working drawings for 1500 sq. ft. residence on level site using manufactured components.

PRESENTATION: Five sheets of hardline pencil drawings on mylar. Refer to job cost summary attached.

DISCUSSION: The production went smoothly except for a delay in the site plan caused by the surveyor. This resulted in some revisions to the sections and the elevations, once the site plan was received. Approximately four additional hours were spent during the check phase.

                 This may be improved in the future through better communications with surveyors provided by the client.

CONCLUSION: The costs incurred are representative for this type of project and may be used to estimate similar ones.

Write a report analyzing each project.

140

Today's client is looking for a clear understanding between he and his Architect regarding design fees. In the past, fees were based on percent of construction cost. Conflicts arise where a project must meet a specified budget, and the designer's input has a great deal of influence over construction cost. There is little incentive to make cost savings efforts when compensation is reduced as the effort succeeds.

Cost based compensation is a method of determining architectural fees based on the cost of doing the design work. Time spent on the project, and the salaries and wages of employees who work on the project, are the major influences. Rent, office expenses, printing costs, and overhead are added in to make up the total cost of providing services. In a competitive market, it is necessary to estimate the amount of design fees, and to make firm commitments based on the estimate. This can be quite risky, especially during the schematic phase of a project with a new client.

Working drawing costs, on the other hand, can be easily estimated. Decisions regarding the extent of the project are usually firm by the time this phase begins, and the amount of effort to produce the drawings is predictable.

Any estimate must begin by determining the extent of the work involved. A scope of services form is shown at the end of the Chapter. The items provided by the Architect are checked off, and are used as the basis for his estimate.

Estimated hours for each element are taken from planning and control data compiled by the methods shown in the previous chapter, and entered into the phase worksheet. These are multiplied by compensation costs and an overhead factor to determine in house costs. Consulting fees are added to find the total costs for each element. The sum of the element costs equals the project cost before printing costs and profits are included.

The estimate shown is a simplified one for a small project. More sophisticated techniques and accounting data are needed for complex projects. A full treatise on "Compensation Management Guidelines" is available through the American Institute of Architects, which explains cost based compensation techniques in detail.

SAMPLE: SCOPE OF SERVICES FORM

JOB: B DATE: MAY 31, 1976	BY ARCHITECT	BY CONSULTANT	BY OWNER	NOT PROVIDED
LAYOUT	✓			
FLOOR PLANS	✓			
SCHEDULES	✓			
SITE PLAN			✓	
STRUCTURE		✓		
FOUNDATION	✓			
FRAMING	✓			
SECTIONS	✓			
FIREPLACE				✓
ELEVATIONS	✓			
UTILITY PLANS	✓			
WINDOW DETAILS	✓			
DIMENSIONS	✓			
INTERIOR ELEV.	✓			
DETAILS	✓			
SPECIFICATIONS	✓			
CHECK	✓			

SAMPLE: PHASE WORKSHEET

JOB: B DATE: MAY 31, 1976	ESTIMATED HOURS	RATE	OVERHEAD	IN HOUSE COST	FEES	TOTAL COST
LAYOUT	6	12.00	1.4	100.80		100.80
FLOOR PLANS	18	12.00	1.4	302.40		302.40
SCHEDULES	6	12.00	1.4	100.80		100.80
SITE PLAN						
STRUCTURE					288.00	288.00
FOUNDATION					96.00	96.00
FRAMING					72.00	72.00
SECTIONS	18	12.00	1.4	302.40		302.40
FIREPLACES						
ELEVATIONS	18	8.00	1.4	201.60		201.60
UTILITY PLANS	6	8.00	1.4	67.20		67.20
WINDOW DETAILS	8	12.00	1.4	134.40		134.40
DIMENSIONS	6	8.00	1.4	67.20		67.20
INTERIOR ELEV.	4	8.00	1.4	44.80		44.80
DETAILS	6	8.00	1.4	67.20		67.20
SPECIFICATIONS	8	12.00	1.4	134.40		134.40
CHECK	14	12.00	1.4	235.20		235.20
TOTAL						$2214.40

Estimated hours are determined from the average cost form found in the previous chapter. Multiply by a billing rate and an overhead factor to get the estimated cost.

Changes in the scope of any project are inevitable. Many things are seen quite differently from the way they are interpreted from drawings, thus prompting a change. Human nature, changing conditions, and costs may be the source of other revisions in the work.

It is not practical to revise the drawings and specifications for each change. These are the contract documents and form the basis of bid record and agreement. They must remain in the form that existed when bids and contracts were executed.

Changes in the scope of the work and the contract documents are possible through addendums or change orders. During a bidding or negotiation phase, addendums are used. Once the contract is signed, revisions are documented with change orders.

An addendum is a written and graphic description of a change, which amends the plans and specifications before the contract is signed. An example is shown following the text. Addendums simply describe the nature of the change.

After the contract has been signed, amendments to the contract documents are made by change order. A sample is also shown following the text. A change order describes the proposed revision, shows the cost of the work, states the revised contract price, and is signed by the Architect, the Owner, and the Contractor.

The important thing to remember when making a revision is to document the change explicitly, and to maintain a record of the way things were before the change was made.

NOTES

DATE:

ADDENDUM #1

PROJECT TITLE:

Foundation Note #4   Change typical foundation wall to 8″ thick concrete with 2–#5 Bars top & bottom with #4 @ 12″
each way.

Specification Par. 4q—Delete all stucco.

DATE:

CHANGE ORDER:

PROJECT TITLE:

TO:

You are authorized to make the following change in the subject contract:

Add one 3″ × 6′–8″ solid core mahogany door with frame type "B" and specified
hardware in the basement between the garage and fireplace.

The amount of the contract will be increased by $90.00. Contract total including this change will be $44,590.00.

Contractor's Acceptance	Owner's Approval	Architect
By_____	By_____	By_____
Date_____	Date_____	Date_____

PART FOUR

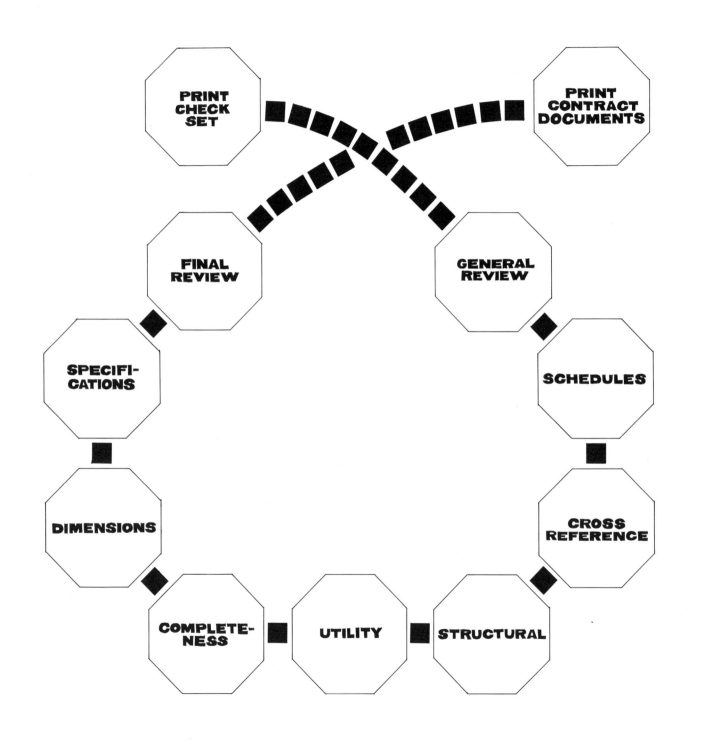

The process described in Part Two has gone through its cycle. A set of drawings and specifications has evolved. They should be relatively complete, but there is no assurance that they are correct.

It is impossible to see the total picture described by the drawings while progressing from step to step. Minor alterations in elements are made which affect other drawings. To stop with each revision and make all the necessary changes is inefficient. Consequently, errors creep in. When more than one person works on the drawings, the problem is magnified.

The importance of the drawings being complete and correct should not be overlooked. In many cases they will become the legal basis for a contract. Ambiguities will manifest themselves on the job, as the contractor proceeds with his work. These are sure to revert back to the architect for clarification, responsibility, or liability.

Checking the drawings can be tedious and confusing. This is best accomplished through process. A person checking the drawings must recycle all of the information through his mind, study the elements from different perspectives, and evaluate their relationship to the total picture of the building.

This should be done by one experienced draftsman, after the drawings are finished. All work on the original sheets should stop. Checking is best done by inspecting a complete set of prints known as the "check set."

The checking process is described by the flow chart and guide provided with this chapter. Correction notes should be marked on the check set at all places where revisions are necessary. When the check cycle is complete, the original drawings should be corrected based on the notes marked on the check set.

CHECK GUIDE

General Review

Check appearance of all drawn elements.

Check each sheet for print clarity.

Check each title block for uniformity and completeness.

Schedules

Review room schedule with:

Plans.

Interior elevations.

Sections.

Review door schedule with:

Plans.

Jamb details.

Elevations.

Sections.

Review window schedule with:

Plans.

Elevations.

Window details.

Cross Reference

Compare floor plans with:

    Elevations.

    Sections.

    Interior elevations.

Compare site plan with:

    Elevations.

    Foundation.

    Sections.

Compare foundation with:

    Elevations.

    Sections.

Compare framing with:

    Floor plans.

    Elevations.

    Sections.

    Ductwork.

    Piping.

    Details.

NOTES

Lighting.

Interior elevations.

Compare utility plans with:

    Floor plans.

    Sections.

    Elevations.

    Framing.

    Interior elevations.

Compare window details with:

    Floor plans.

    Elevations.

    Sections.

    Framing.

Compare details with:

    Framing.

    Sections.

    Foundation.

Structural

Review calculations for:

Proper spans and loads.

Correct data.

Completeness.

Calculation error.

Structural requirements noted on:

Foundation.

Framing.

Connections.

Fabrication information clear for:

Steel columns and beams.

Reinforcing steel.

Glulam beams.

Trusses and joists.

Prestressed concrete.

Utility

Check plumbing and check for:

Code compliance.

Complete baths and kitchens.

Outdoor plumbing.

Frost protections.

Fixtures on schedule.

Check electrical for:

Code compliance.

Convenient switching.

Adequate outlets.

Exterior items.

Fixtures on schedule.

Check heating for:

Compliance with codes.

Complete drawings.

Completeness

Review check lists with:

Floor plans.

Site plan.

Foundation.

Framing.

Sections.

Fireplace.

Elevations.

Utility plans.

Window details.

Dimensions.

Interior elevations.

Details.

Dimensions

Check fixed dimensions:

Windows.

Doors.

Stairs.

Closets.

Bathrooms.

Kitchens.

Other.

Check horizontal overlay of:

Bearing partitions.

Columns.

Exterior walls.

Plumbing stacks.

Foundation.

Check sums of dimensions with:

    Overall dimensions.

    Distance between any two parts.

Check vertical dimensions with:

    Floor elevations.

    Bearing elevations.

    Roof slopes.

Coordinate elevations on:

    Floor plans.

    Site plan.

    Foundation.

    Framing.

    Sections.

    Elevations.

    Details.

    Masonry coursing.

Specifications

Review specifications with:

Room finish schedule.

Door schedule.

Window schedule.

Utility plans.

Equipment schedule.

Structural requirements.

Read specifications throughout.

Final Review

Details provided for:

Railings.

Stairs.

Landscaping.

Flashing.

Millwork.

Special features.

Check problem spots:

Shrinkage points in wood.

Potential flashing leaks.

Ready every note on drawings.

No other task accomplished in a design office is as tedious and exacting as producing a set of working drawings. This Handbook has recommended organizing the work so that its total scope can be seen before beginning; it has encouraged adopting sound working habits so that each step may proceed in a logical order and be completed as it is encountered; and it has shown how to thoroughly check the work so that the drawings produced are clear, complete, and correct.

In short, the text has described how to structure input to make the most out of the energy expended in producing working drawings. Hopefully, this will help a draftsman to understand his role more clearly, to do the work with much less effort, and to find more satisfaction as he works along.

When utilizing this technique, the drawings produced will be well conceived, clearly communicating design ideas to those who will execute the construction work.

Part Two of the Handbook depicts one person working on a residential project, perhaps not the norm for most design offices, and only a beginning description of the scope of working drawings theory. It has been set up this way so that a draftsman can follow through a small project, step by step, and learn the basics. In doing the job alone, he will become aware of the total scope of the work in most projects.

Having learned the basic process, the draftsman then steps naturally into team drafting. As larger, more complex work is encountered, more people and more sophisticated techniques will be utilized.

Persons who have studied the process and have participated in team drafting will be better prepared to deal with more complex works, since they will be able to see how their contribution relates to the whole.

CONCLUSION

American Institute of Architects, *Architect's Handbook of Professional Practice*, A.I.A., Wash. (Revised, June 1974).

American Institute of Architects, *Compensation Management Guidelines for Architectural Services*, A.I.A., Wash. (Feb. 1975).

American Institute of Architects, *Comprehensive Architectural Services—General Principles & Practice*, McGraw-Hill, New York (1965).

American Institute of Architects, *Creative Control of Building Costs*, McGraw-Hill, New York (1967).

Architectural Record, *Techniques of Successful Practice*, McGraw-Hill, New York (1975).

California Council, The American Institute of Architects, *The Techniques of Professional Liability Loss Prevention*, Colorado Society of Architects (Reprinted July 1975).

Coulin, Claudius, *Step by Step Perspective Drawing*, Van Nostrand Reinhold Co., New York (1966).

Halprin, Lawrence, *The R.S.V.P. Cycles: Creative Process in the Human Environment*, George Braziller Inc., New York (1969).

Jones, Christopher J., *Design Methods*, Wiley—Interscience, Wiley & Sons Ltd., London (1970).

REFERENCES